TURNS

WHERE BUSINESS IS WON AND LOST

STEVE McKEE

TURNS: Where Business Is Won and Lost

For more information about this title or to order other books and/or electronic media, contact the publisher: (888) 821-2999

ISBN:
978-1-7356109-3-1 (hardcover)
978-1-7356109-4-8 (ebook)

Printed in the United States of America

Interior design: Darlene Swanson • Van-garde Imagery

To Jordan, Jonathan, and Sarah,
and the joy of a family complete.

CONTENTS

INTRODUCTION

Straightaways are easy.

It's why they invented cruise control, after all. But "set it and forget it" is a sure way to end up in a heap.

Business is a twisting, turning road, and whether you're plotting the future of your products, your positioning, your profitability, or your people, there is always an element of uncertainty about which direction is best. When Robert Frost saw that two roads diverged in a yellow wood, he was sorry he could not travel both. None of us can.

Wanting to know which way to go is something we deal with every day. Sometimes it's as simple as asking a colleague the best route to a new restaurant or in which conference room an upcoming meeting is taking place. At other times it's as complicated as evaluating a new pricing strategy or designing a remote work policy. It may be wondering whether you should hire someone, fire someone, or change the direction of your company. It might be pondering staffing up or slimming down, investing in a new initiative or divesting an old one, or any of a thousand other decisions large and small that come our way in the course of our careers. Turns are where business is won and lost, because turns are where change happens.

But which road to take? Which turn to make? Those are questions that have bedeviled poets and philosophers from time immemorial and from which no mere businessperson is exempt. Making turns is not only endemic to our jobs, it's part of being human, likely more than any of us have ever realized.

Consider the first five minutes of an average day. We turn to get out of bed as we turn off the alarm, turning our necks to work out the kinks. We turn the corner to get to the bathroom and turn away from the mirror until we can look more presentable. We turn toward the kitchen where we turn on the coffeemaker, turning our heads in anticipation when we hear it beep. We turn the lid to open the creamer and grab a spoon to turn in the mug. When we think it's just right, we gingerly turn the mug on our lips to enjoy that perfect first sip. Then we turn on our TVs or smartphones or laptops to get a jump on the day, or perhaps to avoid the challenging fork in the road we're currently facing. You get the idea.

Some of these turns are physical, some are psychological, and some metaphorical, but it's remarkable that so many happen even before breakfast. If you stop to consider how many turns we make over the course of a twenty-four-hour day, you'll realize they're innumerable. And that's to say nothing of the turning points in business that even the simplest choices we make (or avoid) can cause.

Turns represent moments of redirection. Of opportunity. Of transformation. Some turns we choose, and others are foisted upon us. The turns we make are affected not only by the turns of those around us, but by the turns of others around the world. Not to mention the turns of the world itself as it rotates on its axis and orbits the sun. And there are as many ways to think about turns as there are types of them: past and present, helpful and unhelpful, inadvertent and intentional. Turns can be viewed through a microscope or a telescope and reveal different lessons.

Since nothing can move in a single direction forever, turns, by nature, are about limits. But they're also about overcoming limits. Finding new roads. Setting new courses. In every human turn there is decision and there is destiny. The more we learn about turns, the more we learn about ourselves, and vice versa.

When I was young, I had a bit of a compulsion: every time I turned, I felt like I had to "unwind" by turning the opposite way. It was an odd but, fortunately, passing phase. Though my compulsion has dissipated, my fascination with turns remains as I wonder what keeps spinning tops spinning, how dancers can whirl and twirl without getting dizzy, and why some troubled companies can be turned around while others continue down the road to oblivion.

This book originated, in fact, as an effort to take a deeper dive into corporate turnarounds. Helping struggling organizations right their ships is what my firm does for a living; it is how I've spent much of my career. But the more I examined turnarounds, the more I began learning about turns in general, and I became convinced that they could teach us much about other aspects of business.

The philosopher George Santayana famously said, "Those who cannot remember the past are condemned to repeat it." To that I might add that they're also condemned to missing its most valuable lessons. You've probably never considered, for example, how your corporate culture has been shaped by something as distant as the Protestant Reformation. Or how your employee relations have been affected by the Civil War and its aftermath. Or how the economic context in which all of our companies operate is the result of a series of interrelated turns across the globe over the past thousand years. We are all subject to the bias of the present, as if the way things are today are the way things have always been. Not so, and the turns of the past have much to teach us.

As do the turns of physics. A client of mine is also an airline pilot, and he says there are many parallels between flying a plane and piloting a company. For example, inadvertent stalls are a leading cause of fatal aviation accidents. A single-engine airplane can enter a stall for any number of reasons, but when it does the pilot must resist his instincts to pull up; that will further slow the plane's airspeed and cause him to lose all control. Instead, the airplane should be directed downward, using gravity to increase its velocity and regain lift. Once flying speed has been achieved, the pilot can stop the descent and return to a normal, level flight. Pulling up the nose of a stalled aircraft is a natural reaction, which is why pilots-to-be must learn the real-world implications of such a move. One wrong turn and it's lights out.

This is not a paint-by-numbers business book. It's not a *One Minute Manager* memo. It doesn't presume that history began yesterday, that the past is past, or that the answers are easy. By taking a deep dive into turns in arenas as diverse as science, history, religion, art, culture, politics, and sports, however, it will help you connect the dots between yesterday and today, between the literal and the metaphorical, between those who've gone before you and those who'll come after you, and, vitally, between the challenges your company is facing and the strategies to best address them. It won't tell you what to do, but it will provide helpful insights you can apply as you work your way through moments of transition.

There's an old Hebrew proverb about a man who passed by a field that had become overgrown with weeds, its stone wall broken down. "When I saw it," says the writer, "I reflected upon it; I looked and received instruction."[1] It was just an old field, but rather than ignoring it and walking past, the traveler pondered what he might learn from it.

That describes what we're up to here. No one in leadership gets paid just to sit behind the wheel and monitor the cruise control; our jobs require that we turn questions into answers, problems into solutions, and people, circumstances, and situations around. Knowing where and when to turn—not to mention how—requires of us wisdom and discernment.

When Bugs Bunny ended up somewhere he didn't mean to be, he always said, "I knew I should have taken that left turn at Albuquerque." But he didn't have this book. You do, and it's my sincere hope—writing as I am from Albuquerque—that it equips you to better know which way to go the next time you come to a fork in the road.

All it takes to get started is a turn of the page.

ALL AROUND US

"I look at the world and I notice it's turning."
George Harrison

It was a turning point. I turned down the sheets and turned in for the evening, but my mental wheels wouldn't stop turning as I tossed and turned in bed. There was no turning back, and it turned my stomach to think of what would happen if we couldn't turn a corner. I couldn't afford to turn my back on this, but turning things over in my mind helped me turn the problem on its head and revealed how I could turn the tide. I drifted off to sleep knowing everything was going to turn out all right.

Turns—literal and metaphorical—are all around us. While the short story above is admittedly over the top, the fact that more than a dozen idioms about the topic could be used in a one-paragraph tale demonstrates just how commonly we think in terms of turns when contemplating the circumstances that unfold in life and business. Why is that?

That's what I began wondering as I pondered the various crossroads I have come to over the course of a long career, an even longer marriage, and as an employee, employer, boss, father, husband, friend, author, brother, and every other role I play and relationship I have. We have no idea how much the turns we face today have come about as a result of the turns that happened yesterday.

There are events on which economies have turned, inventions by which industries have turned, and innumerable turns of fate, turns of fortune, plot turns, and table turns that led each of us, often unknowingly, to where we are in our careers and companies—many of which we will explore in the coming pages.

Nor is history our only guide. It's remarkable how the turns we come to in business mirror turns in the physical world. For example, in nature there is no such thing as a completely straight line. That seems like a fitting metaphor for why product rollouts rarely go exactly as planned or financial forecasts are never quite accurate. The nature of turns has much to teach us about the nature of business.

There's even much we can learn from observing the many and various turns around us that are, on the surface, unrelated to business. Drivers make turns, children take turns, and farmers turn the soil. Resolution-makers turn over a new leaf, accomplices turn a blind eye, and unhelpful clerks turn a deaf ear. Wrong turns cause collisions, and missed turns lead to serendipity. You can turn your nose up at something or turn your back on someone. When you're embarrassed, it's likely your face turns red. And just think of all the poems and songs and novels and films inspired by turns.

The more I've learned about turns, the more in awe of them I've become, and the more convinced I am that considering them can, pardon the pun, keep one ahead of the curve. History isn't history without them, nor is the future the future. Turns are, truly, all around us, and each has something to teach us.

So, let's go for a spin through the world of turns, beginning with the basics.

We all learned in grade school that the earth turns all day, every day, and the completion of one full revolution in twenty-four hours is what makes a day a day. In every twenty-four-hour period a single point on the equator travels almost twenty-five thousand miles at more than a thousand miles per hour. At that speed it's incredible that we all don't just fly off into space, but thanks to gravity (more on that later), we don't even notice.

The ancients knew that something had to explain the daily cycle, but no one could prove that it was due to the earth turning on its axis until 1851, when Léon Foucault set a giant brass bob swinging from a 220-foot cable at Paris's Pantheon building. A pendulum can't alter its own motion, so when Foucault's enraptured audience observed that his pendulum was slowly yet steadily changing direction, they could come to no other conclusion but that the earth itself was turning.

Since then, replicas of Foucault's pendulum have been set up at museums around the world. Rebecca Thompson, head of public outreach for the American Physical Society, said of the French physicist's exhibition, "It really started the cultural shift to fundamentally understanding our universe differently."[1] Indeed, it did. And it was a foundational building block leading to industries as diverse as aerospace and telecommunications.

Thanks to many other forebears, some who risked their lives in pursuit of a deeper understanding of how the universe works, we now know that the earth doesn't only rotate on its axis, it also revolves around the sun. Once a year. Every year. That full turn is, in fact, what makes a year a year.

Aristarchus of Samos, a Greek philosopher who lived in the second century BC, is the one who first came up with the "heliocentric" hypothesis of a sun-centered solar system. That was quite a departure from giants like Plato and Aristotle, who were convinced that the earth was the center of the universe. Alas, the world wasn't ready for his theory, and it would take a couple thousand more years before Aristarchus was proven correct.[2]

In the early 1500s, Nicolaus Copernicus went public with his own heliocentric theory, which also made the claim that the size and speed of each planet's orbit around the sun varied based on its distance from it. His 1543 *De Revolutionibus Orbium Coelestium* ("On the Revolutions of the Heavenly Spheres") got him in trouble with both the head of the Catholic Church, Pope Paul III, and the father of Protestantism, Martin Luther. Ironically, Copernicus had dedicated his book to the pope, perhaps to earn his indulgence (last pun—I promise).

This brings up a larger point that relates to all kinds of turns: If you're going to go somewhere no one else ever has, you must be willing to at first be thought a fool. It may only be for ten minutes, until you can explain the rationale behind your crazy idea to your team. It may be for ten months, until you can get a minimum viable product into the marketplace and demonstrate traction. It may be for ten years (the jury was out on Amazon for a long time). Or it may be a lifetime or more before people recognize you were correct. At least we're not burning heretics at the stake anymore.

Not just Copernicus, but Kepler, Galileo, Newton, Luther, Wilberforce, and Einstein—all were willing to be considered fools in their pursuit of truth. Light bulbs. Bicycles. Airplanes. Personal computers. All were ridiculed at first. Absolut Vodka. Southwest Airlines. PayPal. Instagram. All were supposed to fail. Few people took the ideas of Sam Walton, Herb Kelleher, or Fred Smith seriously when they first shared them with the world. But the world is better off because they were willing to lean into a turn that others had not yet recognized.

That doesn't mean there aren't a lot of foolish ideas in business. They no doubt outnumber the good ones (mine certainly have). It's a rare talent to be able to discern between inspiration and impossibility. Most of us are at best hit and miss at it, because no one can see around corners. And no one wants to be scoffed at. But if you're going to lead you must risk it, because one thing is always foolish: assuming that the status quo will continue indefinitely. Change is continuous and accelerating. Business models will be usurped. New ideas must be tried. Ironically, having the courage to be occasionally thought a fool may be the best way to avoid becoming one.

Thankfully, both Aristarchus and Copernicus overcame those fears, so that we can now understand how the earth rotating on its axis once every twenty-four hours and revolving around the sun every 365 days underpins much of how we live, including the rhythms of life related to the four seasons.

Autumn is a glorious time of year where I live. I remember going for a walk one day along a forest trail under a brilliant blue October sky and admiring the dazzling hues of red and gold leaves clinging to tree branches and strewn along the path at my feet. It occurred to me that the reason I could relish the beauty of "fall" is that I knew that trees shedding their leaves was part of a cycle.

Imagine seeing entire forests turning yellow and branches becoming ever more barren with each passing day if it had never happened before—you'd think the world was ending. But because we understand that it's part of an annual cycle, the turning of the leaves is something most of us anticipate and relish. Similarly, many businesses experience seasonality in revenues—retailers make most of their annual profit during the Christmas shopping season, and tax accountants are always busiest in the spring. Knowing this keeps their investors, and their spouses, from panicking.

Thanks to Foucault and Copernicus—and Kepler and Newton and Einstein and many others—we now know that virtually everything in the universe is turning, including not only the planets and sun and solar system but the entire Milky Way galaxy as well—all the gas, dust, stars, and planets that surround us are spinning at 130 miles per second. The only thing that may not be turning is the universe itself, which appears to be forever expanding, the implications of which are themselves dizzying.

What's true of the astronomical is true of the atomic. An atom is the smallest unit of a chemical element; it is comprised of protons and neutrons, which together form a nucleus, and electrons, which spin around the nucleus like the earth spins around the sun. Technically, electrons are so small and move so fast that we don't know for sure that they're spinning, but we do know that they remain in unceasing motion around the nucleus. We're learning more about them every day.

CERN, The European Organization for Nuclear Research, operates the Large Hadron Collider, an underground loop nearly seventeen miles around and five hundred feet below the border of Switzerland and France. Built in collaboration with more than ten thousand scientists, one hundred countries, and several dozen universities and independent laboratories, this giant science experiment is the world's highest energy particle collider. It allows physicists to test the predictions of different theories as well as to uncover a deeper understanding of what goes on at the subatomic level by generating collisions at up to thirteen teraelectronvolts (10^{12} electron volts) of energy as beams accelerate around the seventeen-mile loop in opposite directions. High-speed turns create high-impact collisions, generating high-value information, regardless of the outcome.

That is true of all kinds of turns. They're information. They represent discontinuity, a disruption of equilibrium. When margins turn south, there's a reason. When employee turnover increases, there's a problem. When the economy shows signs of recession, there's trouble ahead. But in many of these cases, a coming turn also spells opportunity—if we're paying attention. Turns are a signal in the noise.

And we would do well to pay attention, because literally everything in the universe is revolving, from the galactically big to the infinitesimally small. Even the DNA molecules found in each one of our cells take the form of a double helix—two strands that wind around each other in an elegant and awe-inspiring spiral, carrying detailed and sophisticated instructions necessary for our bodies to develop, survive, and reproduce. It's no wonder we're so conversant with turns and turning; the software carrying the very building blocks of life is built around them.

Think of all that humans have invented over the last two hundred years because of what we've learned about the principles of turning. Ferris wheels. Sprinkler heads. Food processors. Ceiling fans. Treadmills. Industrial robots. The internal combustion engine. The list may not be endless, but I challenge anyone to complete it.

Nobody knows exactly when the wheel was first developed, but we see evidence of its impact throughout human history, from its use in the construction of the Great Pyramids of Egypt to the invention of the wheelbarrow in ancient Greece. In 1817, a German inventor named Karl von Drais introduced the "swift-walker," the first rudimentary bicycle that had a wooden frame, two wooden wheels with iron rims, and leather tires (alas, no pedals). In an ironic twist of history, absent a German inventor, there may have been no Tour de France.

When they weren't busy building one of the seven wonders of the ancient world, the Egyptians were inventing the first time-keeping devices, shadow clocks. These were giant sundials that used fixed obelisks to track the movement of the sun as it (actually, the earth) turned. The first mechanical clocks didn't show up until the fourteenth century, but knowing that the hands of time never stop turning has guided—some would say driven—our lives ever since.

The compass was invented sometime between 200 BC and AD 100 during the Han Dynasty in China. Compasses work by allowing a free-rotating needle to align itself with the earth's magnetic field and reveal magnetic north—and therefore south, east, west, and twenty-eight other points around the circle. At first it was more of a curiosity used for divination and fortune-telling, but by the twelfth century the turn of the compass needle was being used to guide the turning of ships, which, until then, had relied on orientation by the sun and stars. Now seafarers could more safely navigate the oceans, even under overcast skies, which affected everything from migration to commerce to war.[3]

The invention of the steam engine marked the beginning of our modern economy's most significant turn, the Industrial Revolution, which revolutionized transportation, manufacturing, urbanization, family formation, and virtually every other aspect of culture and society. This led to the birth of the Information Revolution, which some argue has eclipsed it in significance. It was only a little more than a century ago that the turn of a propeller put the Wright brothers in flight, which led to the jet engine, which led to orbiting satellites, which enable the instantaneous transmission of information around the globe. If any of us were to trace back the various innovations in our own industries that have led to where we are today, we would no doubt find many common forebears. Every company is a cousin of all others.

Turns are everywhere—not just in business, but in other avenues of life as well, all of which can teach us something. Dancers, drivers, and discus throwers turn on the stage, track, and field. Skiers and skateboarders turn tricks on slopes and in skateparks. Pitchers, quarterbacks, and point guards spin the ball to impact its trajectory just so. Potters use the spinning wheel to shape the clay, while cutlers use it to sharpen the blade. And philosophers, politicians, and diplomats use their skills of rhetoric and negotiation to affect the turn of events. History would hardly be history without turning points.

Some turning points are instantaneous. For all of human history until 1954, nobody had ever run a four-minute mile. The *Daily Telegraph* once called the feat "sport's greatest goal," and physiologists warned not only that it was impossible but that it would be dangerous to a runner's health. Yet on the breezy day of May 6, 1954, Roger Bannister made four turns around Oxford University's Iffley Road track and clocked in at 3:59.4.

"Doctors and scientists said that breaking the four-minute mile was impossible, that one would die in the attempt," he later remembered. "Thus, when I got up from the track after collapsing at the finish line, I figured I was dead." Interestingly, within a month, Australian John Landy bested Bannister with a time of 3:57.9 seconds, and over the course of the following three years more than a dozen additional runners broke the same barrier. Today, high school boys regularly turn in sub-four-minute-mile times.[4]

Other turning points aren't so sudden. Martin Luther nailed his ninety-five theses to the Wittenberg Church door on October 31, 1517, a date that Protestants mark as one of history's most significant milestones. But the Reformation, as this turn has come to be called, comprises a much longer series of events that have shaped so much of our cultural milieu that, like the proverbial fish who fails to recognize the water in which it's swimming, we aren't even aware of it.

The Reformation, simply defined, refers to the period and process by which much of Catholic Europe became Protestant. At the beginning of the sixteenth century, virtually all of Europe had been Catholic. There were a lot of different cultures and forms of government among its roughly sixty million people, but "from the top of Finland to the tip of the boot of Italy, they all had a Latin Mass," says Tia Kolbaba, an associate professor in the Rutgers University Department of Religion who specializes in Medieval Studies. "The Reformation shattered that," Kolbaba says, "and if that's not a turn I don't know what is."[5]

Just as our modern era is marked by rapid technological change, the early 1500s saw a significant transformation of the relationship between the religious and the political. Religion and politics had been inextricably intertwined for all of human history up to that point. There was no separation of church and state; in fact, church and state played together—sometimes well, sometimes less so—in a kind of mutually protective dance.

Alec Ryrie, generally considered one of the Reformation's greatest scholars, says of this time:

> Instead of rivals, the spiritual and temporal powers were generally collaborators: staffed by members of the same great families, sharing the same ambitions for godly good

> order. The temporal powers were the Church's indispensable guardians and patrons. The spiritual power was the monarchs' indispensable reservoir of legitimacy and of bureaucratic expertise.[6]

That said, over the previous two hundred years, the Catholic Church's power had been weakening, at one time having to navigate conflicts brought about by having multiple CEOs (popes). Various reform movements had cropped up throughout the Middle Ages, which the church made a habit of either taming or suppressing. As Ryrie puts it, "If there was a single pattern to these myriad reforming initiatives, it was a cycle in which formality, laxity, habit and corruption was periodically challenged by new or revived movements of invigorated discipline and holiness."[7] Sounds like many of the companies I've consulted, which alternate between periods of focused success and seemingly inevitable mission drift. It's hard to stay on task.

Nevertheless, by the early 1500s, an irreversible turn had been set in motion. Says Ryrie, "This cycle of holiness and laxity was . . . a spiral, not a circle. With each turn, its scope widened from the clerical and monastic elite to the population at large."[8]

This was unnerving, not only to church hierarchy but to the average peasant as well. The pace of change throughout those centuries is not what it is today; life had been more about predictability than progress. Megan Armstrong, associate professor of history and a specialist on Early Modern Catholicism at McMaster University, says, "Going into the sixteenth century if you talked about change, that was a negative term. Change was about destabilization; it was about loss. It was about corruption—corrupting the existing order. The word *novel* in that period meant something new, but *new* meant 'corrupted,' like 'this is threatening.'"[9]

That's why after going public with his somewhat arcane challenges to certain church practices, Martin Luther was hauled before the Diet of Worms and condemned as a heretic. Yet by that time circumstances had turned just enough that Luther would not be burned at the stake as his predecessors had been, and the turn we now call the Reformation became as inevitable as it was consequential. Says Armstrong:

> The Reformation needs to be understood as the product of a confluence of factors that had been building for a long time. People who were in the midst of it, particularly 1520–1550, were aware that they were in something profoundly shifting. You really get the sense of disorientation, excitement, fear, and nothing stable—it was very destabilizing, but not necessarily negative. People were trying to figure out, "What can this new world be? Or should be? Or are we losing? Is change good or bad?"[10]

That last question is one that afflicts every generation. One of the metrics my company measures when we're helping clients understand their internal cultural dynamics is the extent to which they embrace change. Most say they do, but when change comes for them, it can be difficult to accept. Especially when they're uncertain whether a given change will be helpful or harmful. As one focus group participant remarked when asked why he was hesitant to switch to an improved health plan, "I think that's a better canoe than the one I'm in, but I'm not sure I want to make the trip."

The same thing could have been said by a sixteenth-century serf (though probably not in a focus group). The Reformation was both exhilarating and terrifying to those who were living it, but it wasn't the only thing that was changing. A turn in the economy was happening as well.

"The economy" is not a term anyone would have used six hundred years ago. As with politics and religion, the economic conditions at the time were taken for granted. The way things were were simply the way things were. These were the days of feudalism, which lasted for a thousand years after the collapse of the Roman Empire. With the benefit of hindsight, we can look at feudalism with disdain, but at the time it made some sense as an economic system.

For most of prehistory, economic life basically involved hunting, gathering, and rudimentary farming, all subject to the vagaries of climate, weather, soil, disease, and competition from other families and tribes. Some three thousand years before Christ, centralized civilizations began to appear in places like Egypt, China, and the Middle East, and with them came rudimentary economic advances, including record-keeping, banking, and basic business ethics such as those articulated in the circa-1800 BC Code of Hammurabi.

The emergence of the state brought with it some measure of stability, but it also brought the power of the lash, as growing empires depended in large part on slave labor, whether from their own people or from captives taken as the spoils of war. From the pharaohs of Egypt to the prefects of Rome, markets and trading began to emerge even as significant numbers of people were kept under the yoke.

The Roman Empire lasted for more than a thousand years, but not even mighty Rome could forestall a turn indefinitely. In AD 410, the Visigoths finally breached the city's walls, looting, pillaging, and burning their way across it. Following that event, waves of more Visigoths, along with Vandals, Angles, Saxons, Franks, Ostrogoths, and Lombards, carved up the empire, and in AD 476, the last Roman emperor, Romulus, was overthrown. Creative destruction is nothing new.

Then came the early Middle Ages, sometimes derogatorily referred to as the "Dark Ages." It wasn't as if culture, literature, and learning "went dark" during this time, but with political and cultural chaos all around, it was a difficult time in which to get along economically. Roman-era trade routes shrank, Roman roads deteriorated, and the *Pax Romana* gave way to broad lawlessness and power struggles between competing factions and families.

It was in this environment that the feudal system arose. With no imperial ruler to protect (or enslave) them, peasants became tied to the land as serfs, protected by lords of their manor, who were in turn loyal to and protected by various kings. As miserable as the life of a serf could be, it beat going about life alone and unprotected; E. Ray Canterbery, author of *A Brief History of Economics*, says, "In feudal society the serfs worked, the warriors fought, the clergy prayed, the lords managed, and the king ruled."[11] Not ideal, but certainly better than the alternative.

During the time of the Reformation, however, the feudal system began to turn as well, though it remained a long way from the (mostly) free markets and reasonably steady economic growth we enjoy today. As former Federal Reserve Chairman Alan Greenspan points out, "From the birth of Jesus until 1820 . . . economic growth was eleven percent—not per annum, not per decade; per century."[12] But the seeds were being sown for the emergence of Enlightenment economic philosophers, most notably Adam Smith, who would begin to opine on what makes for the wealth of nations and why. It took hundreds of years for feudalism to fade, but once the turn began there was no stopping it.

Just as the old children's song says the foot bone's connected to the ankle bone and the ankle bone's connected to the leg bone, the turns represented by the Reformation and the decline of feudalism are connected with one another—and both are connected to the Civil War and its aftermath, whose long-term effects we're still navigating today.

At the time of Adam Smith, the American economy was effectively two different economies—industrial in the North, agrarian in the South; capital-driven in the North, labor-driven in the South; free labor in the North, slave labor in the South. A reckoning was inevitable.

The then-new United States Constitution hadn't specifically addressed the elephant in the room at that time, slavery. Despite being a slaveowner himself, Thomas Jefferson included a condemnation of the practice in his initial draft of the Declaration of Independence, but in his recollection after the work of the Continental Congress was complete, he said, "The clause . . . reprobating the enslaving the inhabitants of Africa, was struck out in compliance to South Carolina and Georgia, who had never attempted to restrain the importation of slaves, and who on the contrary still wished to continue it."[13]

More than a decade later, when James Madison went to work drafting the Constitution, intense divisions between the delegates of free and slave states would again prevent any consensus on slavery's preservation or abolition. They compromised on Article 1, Section 9, which prohibited the federal government from limiting the "Migration or Importation of such Persons as any of the States now existing shall think proper to admit" until 1808, opening a window to abolish the slave trade that ultimately came to pass at that time.

This feature of the Constitution, along with Jefferson's soaring moral assertion in the Declaration of Independence that "all men are created equal and are endowed by their Creator with certain inalienable rights," set the nation on a course toward abolition and equal rights for all its citizens. But the turn took time, and having punted the issue down the road, it's unlikely the Founders could have comprehended the horror of coming events.

After all, around that same time in Great Britain, the slavery issue was being hotly debated without widespread violence. William Wilberforce, a member of Parliament and contemporary of America's founding generation, had committed his life and career to the abolition of the slave trade and was working tirelessly to discredit it. "So enormous, so dreadful, so irremediable did the trade's wickedness appear that my own mind was completely made up for abolition," he wrote about the conviction that came to him upon his Christian conversion early in his career. "Let the consequences be what they would: I from this time determined that I would never rest until I had effected its abolition."[14]

Wilberforce introduced abolition bills to Parliament nine times between 1789 and 1805, all of which went down in defeat. But he was nothing if not tenacious, and in 1807 Parliament finally rid the British Empire of the slave trade. Wilberforce then turned his attention to the abolition of slavery itself, and in 1833, just days after his death, Parliament passed the Slave Emancipation Act.

The turn away from slavery in Great Britain required of Wilberforce sustained dedication for decades of his life, but in the U.S. its costs were even greater—some 750,000 American deaths.[15] Shortly after the Civil War, retired Harvard professor George Ticknor wrote that it had created a "great gulf between what happened before in our century and what has happened since, or what is likely to happen hereafter. It does not seem to me as if I were living in the country in which I was born."[16] It was the apex of perhaps the most morally consequential turn in American history.

South Carolina became the first state to secede from the Union on December 20, 1860. But it was not the first attempt at secession. During the Whiskey Rebellion that began in 1794 in Pennsylvania, farmers and distillers committed acts of violence and threatened to secede in protest of a new whiskey tax levied to repay Revolutionary War debt. Things got so bad that President Washington had to send in a federal militia to quell it.

During the War of 1812, Federalists in New England considered the idea of seceding, and in the decades that followed, secessionist threats came from places as diverse as California, Oregon, New Jersey, and New York City. In 1845, not everybody in the independent Republic of Texas was enamored with the idea of becoming part of the United States. The republic did become a state but famously retains its independent spirit to this day.

None of these feeble attempts at secession, however, inflamed the passions to the extent that slavery, and the Southern culture and institutions that surrounded and supported it, did in rending the nation in two. It resulted in four bloody years of war, an inconceivable death toll, and the assassination of a man widely considered to be our greatest president. In the end, the Union had been preserved and four million slaves freed, but the turn was nowhere near complete—and in some respects remains incomplete to this day.

As Civil War historian and associate professor at Middle Tennessee State University Derek Frisby has observed, "History is memory, and memories change. Memories are incomplete. As a nation, it's not wrong to revisit our memories and what those memories mean, but we lack a consensus. I guess there's a reason there's been a book a day written about the Civil War since it started."[17]

As these intertwined examples of the Reformation, feudalism, and the struggle against slavery demonstrate, there is no shortage of sweeping turns in religion, economics, war, or any other aspect of our shared history. They intrigue us because their outcomes were the result of unfolding and often unpredictable events. And they are of value to us not only in deepening our understanding of our common history and heritage, but in revealing much of the "why" behind the "what" of the turns we face today.

Who can say how much of today's employer-employee compact—both implicit and explicit—is derived from the causes and consequences of the Reformation? How much do we presume upon the "invisible hand" of the market, which only in the last few centuries has largely been set free from its feudal and mercantilist shackles? To what extent is the cultural tension we experience today related to the unfinished business of the founding and Civil War generations? These are big questions without simple answers, but understanding the context in which we do business (and life) will make us more adept as we write our own chapters of this continuing saga.

Storytelling is an apt metaphor, because turns are found in every literary work of art. Authors of novels, plays, movies, and even advertisements mimic real life by creating narrative arcs that move along familiar and relatable paths. They begin with stage setting, then rising action that leads to some sort of climax, followed by falling action and resolution. Romantic comedies, for example, all seem to follow a similar arc of boy meets girl, boy and girl fall in love, boy does something stupid, girl realizes that it's all a misunderstanding, boy and girl live happily ever after. Within each major story arc there are often minor arcs involving individual characters or events.

Story arcs are turns that keep audiences engaged. Modern television series ensure that the falling action and resolution of one story arc is intertwined with the rising action of another, creating "cliffhangers" that compel us to keep tuning in from one episode to the next. The narrative arc is the basic format followed by all great storytellers, from William Shakespeare to Walt Disney. Without a turn, there is no story. With one, there can be magic.

When Elvis Presley first appeared on *The Ed Sullivan Show* on September 9, 1956, the teenagers who loved his music—and their disapproving parents—had never seen anything like it. The way he sang, the way he moved, and his raw energy told a story they had never seen before. It represented a turn in music, and culture, for which nobody was prepared, and the entertainment business would forever be changed.

A decade later, bold and braggadocious Muhammad Ali became "the first truly modern athlete," boasting to *Sports Illustrated*, "I've left the sports pages. I've gone onto the front pages."[18] He turned the sports business upside down. So did Simone Biles, the undisputed greatest gymnast of all time, fifty years after Ali. Biles's unprecedented strength and near-perfect technique gave her the power and torque to pull off things like the "Triple Twisting Yurchenko" on the vault and the "Biles" in the floor exercise—a gravity-defying double backflip with three twists. It's one of four gymnastic moves named after her that must be seen to be believed.

Fortunately, they can be watched over and over on the web, thanks to an obscure UCLA professor named Leonard Kleinrock who, on October 29, 1969, sent a two-letter dispatch to the Stanford Research Institute's Bill Duvall, marking the first time an electronic message was transmitted over what would become the internet. He was attempting to type "login," but the system crashed before he could get to the "g." It nevertheless set off a turn of events in business (not to mention politics and culture) the implications of which we are still only beginning to grasp.

I recall the first time I heard about the internet, in a conversation over pizza with a couple of engineer buddies. I was only half-listening to them as they talked about exchanging information over some arcane network, certain that there was nothing they were saying that would be of interest to me.

I should have paid more attention. A year or so later, I went to an exclusive industry conference where Ted Leonsis was the featured speaker. Leonsis is best known today as the owner of several professional sports franchises in Washington, D.C., but back then he was a senior executive at a little company called America Online. I was intrigued enough by what he said that I went home and set up an AOL account, but not so much that I invested in the company. That was a mistake.

I'm not the only one to miss a turn in business. Ford dismissed Lee Iacocca along with his crazy idea for what would become the minivan, so he went to Chrysler and changed the automotive business forever. Apple responded to disappointing sales of the Macintosh by firing Steve Jobs, only to see him return years later and make Apple the world's first trillion-dollar company. Kodak invented, and shelved, the digital camera.

Blockbuster turned down the opportunity to purchase Netflix. IBM, Lego, Ford, Hewlett-Packard, Starbucks, Caterpillar, and Xerox have all made wrong turns—some more than once. It's the rare startup that gets it right the first time; most turn (pivot) when their original business models don't pan out.

Ken Chenault is the former CEO of American Express, a company that has itself had to overcome many challenging turns since its founding in 1850. He says, "Enduring companies are not one-trick ponies. Companies with a long-term vision must accept that as the market changes around them, systemic transitions—transformations—are a fact of life. What was once novel becomes a commodity over time."[19]

That sounds like a principle from physics. The second law of thermodynamics deals with a property called entropy, the phenomenon that everything in the universe tends toward disarray. You might say that it's natural for things to take turns for the worse in business. That has certainly been my experience.

That's what happened to Sundt Corporation, a $1.5 billion construction company that has had a hand in building everything from the Apollo launch pad to Austin Bergstrom Airport to Dallas's Reunion Tower and the Walter Cronkite School of Journalism. Sundt built the bulk of the Manhattan Project in Los Alamos, re-created the London Bridge in Lake Havasu City, Arizona, and constructed a major ride at Sea World. Clearly this was a company that knew what it was doing.

Founded in 1890 by a Norwegian immigrant named M.M. Sundt, the company thrived under multiple generations of leadership, particularly during America's postwar boom years. Then suddenly, seemingly without warning, it was heading over a financial cliff. Why? Like many successful organizations that can be lulled to sleep by a long, straight, and smooth road, Sundt's leadership became arrogant and didn't see the need to change. They started taking risks that were beyond their skill sets. That got them into trouble, and the company's new management team wasn't prepared for what would come next.

According to Doug Pruitt, the newly installed CEO at the time, "It was more like a collision than a turn."

Pruitt had started at Sundt as a field agent and had worked his way up the ranks through numerous roles over several years. "I watched Sundt do some marvelous things," he said of his time working his way up the ladder. "And I watched them lose a boatload of money."[20]

The company had lost its focus on running a business and became mired in several legal disputes. There was no organizational consistency. No sense of where the enterprise was headed. No vision, no mission, and enough debt to sink the corporation without immediate write-offs. How could such a successful operation have degenerated so much?

"If you are in business, the answers will be familiar to you," Pruitt said. "Lack of discipline, lack of focus, lack of organizational consistency, lack of employee training, poor succession planning, lack of investment in technology and education, and other familiar tunes sung by companies that fail (or come close to it)."[21]

Richard Condit, the company's then-new senior vice president and chief administrative officer, says of that time, "Planning at Sundt had been nearly nonexistent, at least corporately. We were simply an opportunistic company, pursuing and building construction projects with little thought about risk, profit potential, etc." He went on: "Somewhere along the way, Sundt put its checklist aside and said, 'We've got this.' And unfortunately, this type of arrogance sent the company into a downward spiral."[22]

A downward spiral is not the type of turn in which any company wants to find itself. Yet many do, as do slumping athletes, politicians who make promises they can't keep, and couples that neglect their marriages. "Somewhere along the way" we lose sight of the fact that the straight and smooth stretch of road we're enjoying is the exception, not the rule. We can't always know when the next turn is coming, but remaining alert to it can be a lifesaver.

Daniel Findley knows something about saving lives. He has a PhD in civil engineering and is a licensed professional engineer. He's also an adjunct professor in the Department of Civil, Construction, and Environmental Engineering at North Carolina State University and associate director at the Institute for Transportation Research and Education. As the author of *Highway Engineering: Planning, Design, and Operations*, you might say Daniel wrote the book on road safety.

When it comes to literal turns, Dan is the man. As he puts it, "I'm a curve guy. I'm obsessed with taking pictures of curves because that was my dissertation. I took seventy-five hundred pictures on our [three-week vacation through Wyoming and Idaho] and probably three thousand are transportation related. That's what I enjoy."

We may feel sorry for Daniel's kids ("What, Dad, we're stopping *again*?") but we can be grateful for his wealth of know-how about road design. "Given the choice," he says, "[engineers] will always build a straight line. And you see that in states that don't have many obstructions. The roads are perfectly straight. That's what we prefer. Much more simple."[23]

And safe. While intersections are the most common location of automobile crashes, curves are a close second. They're especially dangerous on two-lane roads—more than twice as likely to result in a fatality.

This was brought home to me all too viscerally one dark night as I drove the twists and turns of Atlanta's Chastain Road. It was the night before a wedding in which I was the best man, and the maid of honor and I were following the bride and groom to the rehearsal dinner when a teenager who had been drinking was coming the other way and crossed the yellow line. He hit us head-on.

I can only imagine what the soon-to-be-married couple were thinking when they turned their car around and sped back to the site of the crash, expecting to find their dear friends in no state to stand in a wedding—or worse. By the grace of God, we were both OK, though not without some bumps and bruises. It had all happened in an instant, simply because the other driver mismanaged a curve.

Findley works to prevent collisions like that, speaking unassumingly about tangents and traverses, arcs and radii. ("A straight line has an infinite radius," he says, matter-of-factly. "Yes, and the universe is continually expanding," I want to shoot back, just to show off.) He explains the Long Chord, the straight-line distance between the turn's point of curvature and point of tangency. And he highlights an important part of most curves, superelevation, which refers to the level of banking in a turn.

Most drivers never notice that highway turns are banked, particularly on interstates, which have been designed to smooth out variations on both straightaways and turns. But on winding mountain roads, there's no way to miss them. The higher the speed and the tighter the radius, the more help the driver needs in navigating the turn; hence, more superelevation.

Findley told me about the Tail of the Dragon, a stretch of U.S. 129 connecting North Carolina and Tennessee and bordered by the Great Smoky Mountains. It's famous for having 318 curves in an eleven-mile stretch and as a result is a popular motorcycle and sports car road. Without careful attention to superelevation and other aspects of road design—including frequent signs warning of speed limits and upcoming curves—the Tail of the Dragon would be notorious for something more than fun.

Professor Findley gave me new respect for the engineers who have developed best practices over decades to keep drivers safe. Unlike clearly marked roadways, however, most turns in business come with no pre-posted warning signs. We must look for signs ourselves, whether it be metaphorical moss growing on the side of a tree or skid marks left on the pavement by those who've gone before us.

That's why examining a broad swath of examples of turns throughout science and history, in art and religion, on the battlefield and the playing field, can be so helpful—fateful turns and their consequences are part and parcel of every human endeavor.

They can be long-arc meta-turns like the unfolding of the Reformation or the evolution of a free market economy. They can be macro-turns that happen over the course of generations like the abolition of slavery or the rise and fall of an industry. They can be mini-turns in the lives of our companies or communities on which each of us can make a significant impact. Or they can be micro-turns like flipping a switch, snapping our fingers, or turning up the corners of our mouth (smiling) at someone in the hallway—the kinds of things we do dozens of times a day without even realizing it. It's remarkable how much they all have in common.

Take a few minutes to reflect on the turns your company has experienced. What is the long arc of the industry in which you operate—how, when, and why did it begin? Where has it been going? What is your place in it? Taking a step back to understand the century-plus history of my field helped my company to see how competitive and commoditized it had become. It also helped us to recognize why for years we had reflexively done so many of the things we were doing, many of which were unhelpful to both clients and staff.

What are the macro-turns to which you've had to adjust, or to which you may currently be adjusting? I can think of a handful of events in the years since my firm was founded—external turns such as the maturation of digital marketing and economic peaks and troughs, and internal turns, including one that led to a corporate near-death experience. Anticipating and preparing for coming turns now plays a key role in our strategic planning process.

What are the micro-turns—the everyday decisions you make without much thought? Your company's policies, procedures, customs, and routines may seem insignificant with respect to their individual impact, but just as sowing an action can ultimately reap a destiny, the slightest of turns, by definition, will always change your course. It's not unreasonable to suggest that the extent to which you're off track can be traced back to turns you, intentionally or inadvertently, made. Or failed to make.

Even with life's predictable turns like the changing of seasons, the sweep of a secondhand, or pages turning over on a calendar, nothing remains exactly as it was. In that sense, turns can be strangely encouraging because they infer causality; where there's a turn, there's a *reason*. Becoming more alert to the turns all around us can help us grasp what may be happening and make better decisions at the crossroads to which we come.

Some turns happen to us. Some happen by us. Some we should fear. Some we can relish. Some represent opportunity we can choose to embrace. Some represent limits we're forced to accept. We can't avoid them, but we can lean into them. No turn, no matter how distant it seems in time or space, is irrelevant. The more we embrace the inevitability of turns, the better able we'll be to help our organizations master them—or at least prevent being mastered by them.

In the following chapters we'll explore what all turns—historical, physical, and metaphorical, meta, macro, and micro—share in common, and uncover lessons that will enable us to better understand their nature. Because one thing is certain: there's always another turn around the corner.

The Principle All Around Us

Turns are as commonplace in business as they are in life.

The more we understand them, the better we'll navigate them.

OBJECTS

"Turn the page."
Bob Seger

From figure skaters and ice cream makers to propellers in the ocean and planets in motion, things turn. Beyond physical things, however, life turns in innumerable ways. Turns are simply the way of things in science, in war, in economics, in culture, in sports, in health, in families, and yes, in business. Given the incredible diversity of circumstances and environments in which we can observe turns, it's odd that we use a single word to characterize them all. What could all these turns possibly have in common?

Quite a bit, believe it or not. In the coming chapters we're going to explore a half-dozen characteristics that are true of every type of turn—historical, physical, and metaphorical—beginning with the most basic: from the atomic to the astronomic, by itself or as part of a larger ecosystem, one way or another, everything turns. It therefore follows that every turn requires a thing.

That sounds obvious, but in it lies the first key to better navigating the choices with which we're continually faced: the ability to mentally separate the turn itself from that which is turning—especially when the latter is *us*. Otherwise, we risk letting our emotions derail us.

I discovered this the hard way when, after five years of rapid growth following its launch, my firm inexplicably stalled. There had been no bolt of lightning, no aggressive new competitor, no recession on which to put the blame. But our revenues were flat and beginning to decline, and nothing I did to try and correct the situation seemed to have any impact.

To add embarrassment to injury, we had recently made the *Inc. 500* list of the fastest-growing private companies in America. I attended the awards conference with my tail between my legs; here I was, sitting in roundtable discussions with CEOs of companies that were dealing with the need to hire dozens of people, finance their expansions, and mature their operations, and I could do little more than stare at my shoes. The last thing I wanted was to participate in the conversation, as I would have either had to misrepresent the truth or confess that I was an imposter.

It was that imposter syndrome that delayed our recovery. I suppose I had given myself too much credit on the way up, thinking I was more responsible for our success than I had been. I only later learned that I blamed myself too much on the way down.

Not knowing what else to do, several months into the stall, we leveraged our status as an *Inc. 500* member to survey other companies that had made the list over the preceding twenty years. We discovered that nearly one in five had run into rough waters similar to ours. It was only then I realized that perhaps our struggles were due less to inept management than to normal growing pains. Once I was able to separate the object of the downturn, my company, from my performance as its leader, I could dispassionately evaluate what to do about it. It only cost me a year before I figured that out.

It can be difficult to separate subject (us) from object (our companies) when we come to turns. Think about it: a change in direction, by definition, represents something new; new things are unfamiliar, unfamiliar things are risky, and risky things are frightening. In the midst of a turn, just when we need to be levelheaded in our evaluation of what's happening, our emotions can gum up the works, often without our realizing it. That can lead to some bad decision making, not to mention an ulcer.

Partly as a result of this experience, I created a pithy mantra that relieved me from worrying so much about unfortunate turns in my professional life: "Not my fault, is my problem." In my line of work (likely yours as well) things go wrong every day, and one way of understanding my role is that it's my job to fix them. But being responsible for fixing problems is very different from having caused them, which in most cases is not a charge that can be laid at my feet; I'm pretty good at my job. As a conscientious person, however, bearing the emotional weight of the problem is an involuntary and subconscious burden. The better I have been able to separate the object (me) from the turn (the problem), the better able I am to think clearly about solutions. And sleep more soundly.

Our ability to disassociate objects from turns increases the likelihood that we will make our decisions based on the true nature of things rather than on subjective emotions. Cultivating the ability to distinguish the two is good practice. To cite an example so obvious you've probably never thought about it, we casually refer to curves in the roadway as "turns," but they're merely nonlinear distributions of asphalt or concrete. They don't become "turns" until something turns on them. In the same way, an orbit is an orbit only when something is orbiting, and an axis is an axis only when something is rotating upon it.

Which, as it turns out, is a necessary thing for life on this planet. "If the world stopped turning" may be a terrific title for a love song, but if it happened in real life things would quickly get highly unpleasant. If for some reason the object we call "earth" stopped rotating, scientists tell us that the oceans would recede away from the equator toward the poles, creating a single continent that circumscribes the globe, separating two giant polar oceans.

That sounds kind of interesting and worth exploring, but since half the planet would continually face the sun and half the dark of space, most of the earth would be unlivable. Life could theoretically survive on the margins between the two halves, but as we continued our annual turn around the sun, this narrow "biozone" would slowly creep around the world. Whatever civilization there was would have to migrate with it, continually. With little or no sleep, human circadian rhythms would be thrown off entirely—and there would be no coffee to help, because there would be nowhere to grow coffee beans.

Worse, if the stoppage were sudden, the atmosphere would continue whooshing eastward at more than a thousand miles per hour, taking everything on the surface—every rock, every tree, every building, and every person—with it. The earth's magnetic field would decay, causing the awe-inspiring Northern Lights to vanish from sight, along with protection from harmful electromagnetic solar storms, giving new meaning to the term "sunburn."

Fortunately, while the rotation of the earth is measurably slowing down, it's doing so by only about 1.7 milliseconds per century. [1] Unlike the slowdowns we all must deal with every decade or so when the economy goes into recession, we can probably move fretting about this unlikely event down our list of priorities.

So much for the axis. What about the orbit? Well, if for some reason the earth stopped rotating around the sun, things would be even worse. It just so happens that the thirty kilometers per second at which our planet is hurtling through space is precisely the right speed to counteract the force of gravity pulling us toward the sun. If the earth stopped in its tracks and we somehow were able to avoid being thrown off into space, the sun would—at first gradually, then with increasing velocity—suck us into its gravitational field. Within about two months, temperatures would hit some 3,800 degrees and the entire planet would be turned to goo.[2] At least we wouldn't have to worry about shareholder meetings.

So, let's hear it for the faithful turns of the objects in our solar system. They not only keep us alive, they keep us on time. Hands turn on a clock because minutes turn to hours. Pages turn on the calendar because days turn to weeks. Each of us turns eighteen, then twenty-one, then twenty-nine, then (it becomes impolite to ask) because one year turns into another. And every hundred years, we witness a turn of the century. Clocks, calendars, years, and centuries all turn because things in our solar system turn.

As does the weather. It would be terrific to be rid of hurricanes—one of the few positive ramifications if the world were to stop rotating on its axis—but turns in the weather are tied to the rain cycle and snowpack and pollination and a host of other climatological effects that enable life. As annoying as blustery breezes can be, they're what spread the seeds and carry the rain and clear the sky. We can appreciate the winds of change in general, even as we're annoyed by those that may be currently blowing our companies off course.

There are many other objects from which we can learn if we pay attention to how they turn. Doors, for example, without which we'd have little privacy. Or light switches, without which we'd be reading by candlelight. Even the pages of a book.

A page is simply a lever we turn to see what's on the other side. We tend not to think in those terms because in a book or a magazine the pages are many, the turns frequent, and the turning subconscious (unless it's a really bad read). A book's binding plays the role of a hinge on which the pages-as-levers turn; if you've ever read a children's story to a toddler, you'll note that part of the experience is the joy the child gets in flipping the pages to see what's on the other side. Without turns, there would not only be no "page turners," there would be no books.

It's even true of e-books, which require nothing more than a flick of the finger at the bottom of each page. Fingers only flick because they have hinges called knuckles, each of which is one of hundreds of synovial (movable) joints in our bodies that operate by turning.[3] Imagine what life would be like without knuckles, shoulders, elbows, wrists, hips, knees, ankles, and toes. If your jaw didn't turn, it would be impossible to chew. If your eyes didn't turn, it would be impossible to cast a sideways glance. And if your head couldn't swivel, there would be no way to rubberneck the next time you pass an automobile accident.

Speaking of which, car wrecks tend to happen in two places: at stoplights, which work by turning from green to yellow to red and back, and on curves. Mercifully, cars have become much safer over the past several years, from the quality of tires to the responsiveness of suspension systems. But drivers have pretty much stayed the same, and we're usually the cause of the problem. As "Curve Guy" Daniel Findley would underscore, safely getting through a turn in the road is at least as much about the driver as it is about the curve. That's why it's such a good metaphor for business.

Road engineers usually design to the 90th percentile of safety, because achieving 100 percent would be impossible ("Our roads would need mattresses alongside them or something," says Findley). They pretty much know what brakes and suspension systems and windshield wipers and other aspects of the objects with which they're dealing can do, and they factor those variables into their equations. But to get to that 90 percent, they must ask a lot of questions about the average driver: How good is their eyesight? How quick are their reflexes? How likely are they to be distracted? How will they know how sharp the curve is? Are they familiar with the road, or new to the area? What are their expectations?

"The curvy road driver expects curves," says Findley, and those on straightaways expect more straightaway. "The research shows that about eight to twelve seconds is what we carry forward in our short-term experience," he says. "So, if they've been driving on a straight [stretch] for more than eight to twelve seconds, they expect to keep going straight." Roadway designers must take that into account.

Findley says that since drivers on a mountain road naturally assume there are going to be a lot of curves, roads are designed accordingly. If engineers create long straightaways that are interrupted by sharp, intermittent curves, they're going to create safety issues. But the same road with lots of little curves? Probably no problem. "The one thing in my highway design class I stress over and over again is drivers' expectations," says Findley. "When we meet drivers' expectations, we generally have positive outcomes, and when we violate drivers' expectations, we have suboptimal outcomes."

My company sees this principle manifest itself in the variety of industries we serve. Companies in the tech industry are like cars on winding mountain roads; before they even complete a turn, they're anticipating the next one. By contrast, companies in industries that change more slowly, such as real estate or insurance brokers, construction companies, and funeral homes, are often surprised and knocked off course by unanticipated turns.

There is a larger principle at work here. Unlike inanimate objects that predictably turn according to universal laws of nature, companies traverse turns in ways that are as varied as they are unpredictable. We can ace turns, blow turns, anticipate turns, or be surprised by turns. We can choose to turn or be forced to turn. But no matter how we respond to them, turns require us to distinguish what must happen from how we feel about it; how well we navigate them is due in part to how dispassionately we can perceive them. "If change is the norm," Findley says, referring to roadway curves in a way that applies just as well to other situations we may face, "you're going to be able to handle turns better."

Handling turns better is something elite athletes spend countless hours practicing, whether on the track, in the gym, or through the water. In the short-course one-hundred-meter freestyle, the men's world record for covering four lengths of a twenty-five-meter pool is under forty-five seconds. That includes three flip turns, which, if not executed perfectly, are where the race almost assuredly will be lost.

A flip turn is one of the most complex movements in sports. The swimmer must judge his breathing and stroke precisely as he heads into the wall at maximum speed, initiating a 180-degree turn while also rotating 180 degrees in less than a second. He must "stick" his turn with feet placed in exactly the right position on the wall to ensure an explosive push off at just the right depth below his own wake, and he must keep his hands above his head in the most aerodynamic position as he executes four or five underwater dolphin kicks prior to breaking the surface with maximum velocity. And do it all in a state of oxygen deprivation. And in a one-hundred-meter short course race, repeat it ten seconds later, and ten seconds after that. A well-executed flip turn is a thing of beauty, but it doesn't happen by chance. It's the result of intent and a great deal of practice.

There is no shortage of examples in sports of the sublimity of turns. The figure skater carving the ice with grace. The gymnast defying gravity. The two-hundred-meter sprinter leaning into the curve. The point guard turning an errant rebound into a fast break. The quarterback lofting a perfect spiral for a touchdown. The infield turning a double play. We love sports because they are a microcosm of life. Whether it's the tragedy of a turned ankle or the momentum that turns defeat into victory, the games we play are most dramatic and engaging when someone, or something, turns. I've often joked that you can explain pretty much anything that happens in business using a sports analogy.

The same is true of other forms of entertainment. Fairy tales wouldn't be fairy tales without the witch turning the prince into a frog or the pumpkin turning into a carriage. Motion pictures were first called motion pictures because the turning of movie reels gave a series of still pictures the appearance of motion. Amusement parks wouldn't be as amusing without the turn of the Ferris wheel, the spinning of the Tilt-a-Whirl, or the loop-de-loop of the roller coaster—and parks have become more amusing now that operators have figured out how to use psychological distractions to make the lines seem like they're moving faster.

This is a good example of a turn any of us might recognize if we just pay closer attention. Amusement parks have always had lines; as long as park owners thought of rides as being their business, waiting in long, hot lines was just what happened in between. However, once operators realized that their object wasn't the intermittent amusement of their guests but rather their uninterrupted enjoyment, anything that soured the experience became fair game for improvement. Makes you wonder what potential turns for the better might be right under our noses.

Turns are powerful in the fashion industry, too, as they're what trends are made of. When I was a kid, bell-bottoms were in. Then they were out. Then in. Then out. Then I gave up trying to remember because I turned old enough not to care. Once upon a time a Burberry trench coat was the height of sophistication. Then it wasn't. Then it was again. Broad fashion trends tend to follow a twenty-five-year cycle, while fads sometimes last for only a season. But both are used by fashion designers to turn a profit.

Turns are even woven into music—more than we likely realize. "Turn" is actually the name of an ornament, or embellishment, in classical compositions. Composers or performers might, for example, "decorate" a note by alternating pitches one step above and one below the main note itself. "For long periods of time in the seventeenth and eighteenth centuries, it was the go-to trick," says music historian Mat Langlois. "It's a way of decorating a note that might otherwise just be sustained, the purpose being to add interest."[4]

Langlois isn't your everyday music fan. He has a PhD in music history from Cornell University and was the former assistant editor of *Keyboard Perspectives*, a journal focused on the history of keyboard instruments and the music they create. He's been a lecturer in music history at multiple universities and won the Paul A. Pisk Prize for Best Doctoral Research Paper from the American Musicological Society. He's an accomplished flautist as well. Mat knows his music.

Though they may have arisen in the classical era, turns are not limited to classical compositions. "Go listen to Adele or any other pop musician in the modern day," Langlois says, "and they'll be doing turns." The notion of coming back or returning is central in a lot of music theory, he says, and movement between keys is responsible for a lot of the tension and resolution that we perceive in music, whether or not we're conscious of it.

A different type of turn is used to set the mood and pacing of many rock-and-roll anthems. Few songs establish a mood better than Ted Nugent's "Stranglehold," whose rhythmic bassline repeatedly turns in upon itself over the song's eight-minute length, or the Outlaws' "Green Grass and High Tides," which begins with a slow tease that sets up nearly ten minutes of circular motion only the finest bass players can master.

Lyrical turns are common as well, as are melodic turns. "Melody—a sequence of pitches—can provide the most basic kind of turn in classical music," Langlois says. In some cases, a melody may even be used to sonically imitate a turn. He says the most famous example may be Schubert's "Gretchen am Spinnrade" (Gretchen at the Spinning Wheel), in which the piano's right-hand melodic pattern mimics the turning of a spinning wheel throughout the piece.

There are turnarounds in jazz, too, which are what enable the musicians to sync up and take turns improvising. "Inserting this little unit called the turnaround, which is itself just a little sequence of chords, is a good way of sort of getting everyone on board—of saying, 'Oh, okay, we've reached the end of this section and we're onto the next one,'" Langlois says. Even audiences perceive it, which is part of how they sense when to start clapping for one of the players in the middle of a piece.

Bridges are a type of a turn in song that can be incorporated to provide a kind of relief from the repetitive alternation of verse and chorus, especially in pop music. Turns in tempo are also quite common, often used to mark a turning point in the song. Think Arcade Fire's "The Crown of Love," which builds slowly and then makes a sudden turn in both tempo and meter at the climactic moment, or Led Zeppelin's "Stairway to Heaven," which gradually increases tempo through many subtle steps, each accompanied by changes in melody and instrumentation.

Speaking of Led Zeppelin, there have been few turns in branding as bold as when Cadillac licensed the band's 1971 anthem, "Rock and Roll," making it the soundtrack of the automaker's newly redesigned fleet of cars. "Rock and Roll" captured the nonconformist spirit of a new generation of car buyers, Baby Boomers, which Cadillac desperately needed to attract to prevent the brand from slowly dying along with its historical customer base, the World War II generation. Juxtaposing what, at that time, was thought of as an "old man's brand" with rebellious kids' music provided just the jolt the brand needed to capture the attention of a new customer base and turn its declining fortunes around.

As the Cadillac example demonstrates, musical turns provide a literal object lesson regarding the Principle of the Object. Musical compositions are uniquely capable of setting an emotional context, from the melancholy of an Adele ballad to the driving intensity of Led Zeppelin, and all feelings in between.

Advertisers and filmmakers are experts at using melody, tempo, and instrumentation to set the emotional tone for a product, service, or scene, using music to manipulate the emotions of their audience. Dispassionately examining it as we are here, it's easy to disassociate ourselves from those effects and see how they work. But in the normal course of life we accept and often embrace how music makes us feel, letting our emotions go where they will. When we come to a turn in business, however, that's exactly what we must not do.

Fred Smith, the founder of FedEx, somehow managed to set his emotions aside when his then-young company was near bankruptcy, its startup capital plummeting from $84 million to $5,000. In a move I wouldn't recommend as a standard fundraising tactic, he flew to Las Vegas and turned $5,000 into a cool $27,000, buying him enough time to raise an additional $11 million in operating funds. Within a few years, the company's bottom line had turned from red to black. Fittingly, the entire FedEx business model is based on turns, as each evening planes from all over the country fly to Memphis, swap packages, and turn right back around again to deliver them the next day.

Cadillac's parent company, General Motors, has gone through several turnarounds, the first time when the market for its vehicles collapsed two years after its founding in 1908. It happened again in 1918, then again in the 1980s with the advent of efficient and affordable imports, then again in 2009 due to the Great Recession.[5] Today GM is doing all it can to not be left behind in the turn to electric vehicles.

Lego lost money for the first time in more than sixty years when it was confronted by an onslaught of new competition from video games and the internet. To make matters worse, the company had tripled the number of toys it produced, averaging five new product releases a year. Many of those launches failed to take off, causing Jørgen Vig Knudstorp, executive chairman of Lego Brand Group, to say, "Right now, our mission is just to survive. To cut costs, sell businesses, and restore our competitiveness."[6] Through an innovative strategy built largely upon refocusing on its core products, fifteen years later Lego had turned itself back into the world's most profitable toymaker.[7]

As these examples demonstrate, turns may be one of the most common metaphors in business. The restaurateur seeks table turns. The grocer pursues inventory turns. The furniture maker turns wood on the lathe before turning the corner in his truck to deliver your new coffee table. All of us try to minimize staff turnover, and due to the vagaries of the marketplace, every company must sooner or later deal with a turn in its own fortunes.

The late Theodore Levitt, formerly a professor at the Harvard Business School and much-heralded editor of the *Harvard Business Review*, summed it up well when he said, "Every major industry was once a growth industry. But some that are now riding a wave of growth enthusiasm are very much in the shadow of decline. Others which are thought of as seasoned growth industries have actually stopped growing. In every case the reason growth is threatened, slowed, or stopped is not because the market is saturated. It is because there has been a failure of management."[8] One failure of management is to forget that your company as it exists today is merely the object, not the objective. It can, and must, change.

It's a truism in business that every industry moves through a cycle of innovation, acceleration, maturation, saturation, and commoditization, and corporate leaders who don't realize this are almost always caught flat footed. It may take a decade (the tech industry) or a century or more (the funeral industry) to see the fallout, but the cycle of invention and destruction never stops turning.

That was the unpleasant fact confronting the new leadership team at Sundt. Doug Pruitt said, "We weren't willing to take a hard look in the mirror. We were afraid of what we might see." By the time he stepped into the CEO role, "the company was mired in a culture where losing was accepted and quickly forgiven. Most people didn't pay much attention to the losses until we were nearly broke."[9]

Perhaps because of his detachment from the previous administration, Pruitt was able to identify issues others couldn't. There are a lot of things about the volatile construction industry that make it difficult to manage, but in Sundt's case he believed most of the issues were self-inflicted and avoidable, including insufficient strategic planning, a lack of corporate discipline, and neglecting the importance of training and development. "If you lose money, most of the time it's because of you," he says. Making matters worse, the company had been giving across-the-board bonuses to its staff, effectively subsidizing the employees of money-losing divisions and rewarding a lack of performance and accountability.

Over the course of several years of success, the company had lost its "shoulder to the wheel" mentality. Jim Collins, author of *Built to Last*, *Good to Great*, and other business bestsellers, writes about a "flywheel effect" in corporate transformations. A flywheel is a heavy, revolving wheel in a machine that provides predictable momentum by storing kinetic energy and smoothing the delivery of power from the motor. It can be difficult to get a flywheel moving, but once it gains momentum it almost becomes self-sustaining. To get to that point, says Collins, requires a great deal of effort, "turn upon turn, building momentum until a point of breakthrough."[10]

That requires of those in charge both determination and perseverance, two things that can be in short supply when they're needed most. Says Sundt's Pruitt, "When you're trying to turn a business around from the brink of collapse, remaining levelheaded can be nearly impossible."[11] But it's essential, and although it became apparent to Pruitt and his new team that creating a positive flywheel effect at Sundt would be difficult and time-consuming, they had no alternative.

It is often in the transition between generations of leadership that organizations run into trouble; there are few situations in business where it's more difficult to think critically and unemotionally, separating object (the worth of the company) from subject (the outgoing and incoming generations of management). So much of our identities are rooted in our careers, and never more so than when people have put years of blood, sweat, and tears into building a company in their own image.

That's why so many succession plans go wrong, particularly in small businesses. Almost 90 percent of companies have fewer than twenty employees, and they create almost two-thirds of all new jobs.[12] Yet statistics show that three-quarters of small businesses fail to survive past the first generation.[13] Nobody lives forever, and the leader of a company has no excuse for not seeing the coming bend in the road. The longer the leader denies or avoids it, the more certain the wreck ahead.

There are several common reasons why succession plans fail, from the inability of the outgoing generation to let go, to greed (on both sides), to starting too late—a good succession plan can take up to a decade or more. False hope can be a problem, too; succession is a complicated process, and it's easy for owners to keep their heads in the sand, hoping an outside buyer will come along or that it will all somehow otherwise work out. There is a thread, however, that runs through all these reasons, and it largely goes unnoticed. Call it an asynchronous view of the turn.

Typically, the outgoing generation is basing its expectations on how they came out of the last turn—thirty-five or forty years of hard work, of figuring out how to make a profit and take care of customers and build a reputation and hire and train and hundreds of other things that go into keeping a going concern going. By contrast, the incoming generation is looking ahead to the next turn, basing the company's prospects not on its impressive past but on an unknowable future. They're trying to continue customer care and keep the company relevant and profitable and growing and thriving, keeping all the cash they can in the business to minimize the likelihood they'll have to manage a shutdown rather than a going concern.

This explains why both sides may be tempted to accuse the other of being greedy, basing their value perceptions on different assumptions. It's the reason the outgoing generation has a hard time letting go of "the way we've always done things," sometimes taking personal offense at the speed with which the new team pursues change. Most organizations hold tightly to their business models and loosely to their value propositions, when precisely the opposite is called for. Especially during moments of transition.

What's true of industries is true of economies. Economies turn through predictable cycles of rapid growth and increasing productivity (expansion) followed by slowing growth and increasing unemployment (contraction), with peaks at the top and troughs at the bottom. While economic turns are predictable, their timing never is, and the irrationality of investors is legendary.

Those who master the timing of an economic cycle—through brilliant analysis or dumb luck—can get rich. But they must be careful, because no two economic expansions and contractions are ever the same, and it can be a short ride from the billionaire's club to bankruptcy court. "History repeats itself as a spiral, not a circle," says Matt Ridley, author of *The Rational Optimist*.[14]

Historian Arthur M. Schlesinger Jr. would agree. In his fascinating book *The Cycles of American History*, Schlesinger opined about "the vicissitudes of presidential reputations":

> The reputation of American Presidents is particularly dependent on the climate in which historians render their verdicts. Judgment is very often a function of the political cycle—that perennial alternation of private interest and public purpose which characterizes American political history.[15]

The political cycle, like the economic cycle—and often tied to it—continually turns. Schlesinger makes a compelling case as to why:

> A generation's political life lasts about thirty years. Each generation spends its first fifteen years after coming of political age in challenging the generation already entrenched in power. Then the new generation comes to power itself for another fifteen years, after which its policies pall and the generation coming up behind claims the succession.[16]

Schlesinger suggests that political turns may be less rational and more related to economic conditions and generational turnover than anything. If we could critically analyze our most deeply held political beliefs and better understand where they came from, we might be less reflexive in our opinions and improve our collective decision making regarding where we want the country to go.

Where the country was going was particularly relevant in the presidential election of 1896, though most Americans are unaware of it. In fact, most of us couldn't name the winning candidate, let alone the losing one, but the outcome was consequential then, and remains so today.

The nation had been experiencing a hangover from the Civil War and the Reconstruction period and had recently experienced a painful economic trough, the Panic of 1893. The Democrat candidate, William Jennings Bryan, built a populist campaign around opposition to the gold standard in favor of silver. At the tender young age of thirty-six, just one birthday beyond the constitutional requirement for a presidential candidate to be no younger than thirty-five, Bryan gave a stem-winding oration that came to be known as the "Cross of Gold" speech. Unfortunately for him, "Gold Bug" Democrats who favored the gold standard united behind the sitting president, Grover Cleveland, and split the vote.

On the other side, Republicans nominated William McKinley, who was known as a friend of both labor and tariffs—issues that would come to be associated more with Democrats than Republicans during the following century. He predictably blamed the country's recent economic problems on his opponents and promised to turn things around. He also had a wealthy financier named Mark Hanna behind him, who raised millions of dollars to purchase mass media advertising in newspapers and magazines in support of the campaign. While Bryan crisscrossed the country, giving more than six hundred speeches while traveling some eighteen thousand miles, McKinley was able to campaign mostly from his front porch.

McKinley handily defeated Bryan, a victory that represents several turning points in American political history. He was the last president to have served in the Civil War. His was the first truly mass media-driven presidential campaign. His election marked the rise of the urban industrial vote at the expense of the rural agricultural vote. And his presidency marked the end of nineteenth-century post–Civil War navel-gazing and political stalemates, and the beginning of the U.S. taking a major role in international affairs, largely due to its decisive victory in the Spanish–American War—one result of which was Hawaii becoming a U.S. territory, a turn for which we can all be grateful.

Ironically, despite McKinley's setting the stage for an unprecedented run of Republican success (winning six of the subsequent eight presidential elections and holding majorities in Congress for thirteen of the following seventeen sessions), the political winds were about to turn again when Teddy Roosevelt ascended to the nation's highest office upon McKinley's tragic assassination in 1901. The Progressive Era had dawned.[17]

War is simply politics by other means, to paraphrase Prussian military strategist Carl von Clausewitz. Over the course of four long and bloody years during the Civil War, President Abraham Lincoln had to navigate many turning points. William Lee Miller, author of *President Lincoln: The Duty of a Statesman*, describes the kind of leader the moment called for with a series of rhetorical questions:

> Could he discern objectively, not deceiving himself with wishes, the actual shape of the concrete reality in which he would make decisions? Could he connect the

> great moral principles to which he had given voice to the severely limiting realities of the actual complicated world he faced? Having made that discernment and that connection, could he decide? Having decided, could he persuade others? Could he lead? Having decided and persuaded, could he hold to his course through vicissitudes? But could he then change—admit mistakes, alter course—when circumstances would warrant?[18]

These are questions we may ask of ourselves when confronted with trying circumstances. In Lincoln's case, to our great fortune, the answer to each of them was yes. Miller goes on to say of his subject, "He had intellectual and moral self-confidence: he had deep conscientiousness, a powerful desire to achieve something worthy, a romantic idea of his country, and an unusual sympathy for creatures in distress. He had a willingness to admit what he did not know and a feel for the way large bodies of human beings were going to respond."[19] Miller points out that James Buchanan, Lincoln's predecessor in the run-up to the Civil War, had held a series of impressive high offices that nevertheless left him "no wiser than he began," while Lincoln prepared himself in small things by simply "thinking all the time."[20]

Lincoln knew that the founding of our constitutional republic was, in the sweep of history, only a recent turn, and by no means a necessarily permanent one. He believed "that ballots are the rightful, and peaceful, successors of bullets; and that when ballots have fairly, and constitutionally, decided, there can be no successful appeal, back to bullets."[21] It's one of many reasons his secretary of state, William Seward, said Lincoln "is the best of us . . . his magnanimity is almost superhuman."[22] Robert E. Lee attributed his surrender of the Confederate Army "as much to Lincoln's goodness as to Grant's armies."[23] Would that people would say something like that about any of us who lead organizations.

Despite Lincoln's strengths as a leader, victory in the Civil War was by no means assured, and the British Parliament nearly came to the aid of the Confederacy, a development that would have almost assuredly turned the tide of the war. As the fateful year 1865 unfolded, however, and Union victory began to coalesce around the armies of Grant and Sherman, Lincoln began to turn his attention to winning the peace.

He was the right person for the job, having a keen sense for the need of the moment and the ability to separate object from incident. "A man has not the time to spend half his life in quarrels," he said. "If a man ceases to attack me, I never remember the past against him."[24] Lincoln was determined to take a mature and measured approach to Reconstruction, "with malice toward none," as he welcomed the Southern states back into a Union he never really regarded them as having left. But for the turn Lincoln's assassin, John Wilkes Booth, chose to take, history may have been very different for all of us.

Just as Lincoln played a pivotal role in the nation's internal divide, Martin Luther played a pivotal role in the church's. But Luther was far from the only, or even the first, key player in the Reformation. There were pockets of people raising similar issues from the fourteenth century onward, including Jan Hus and William Tyndale, both of whom would be martyred for their stances.

And there were many attempts at reform within the Catholic Church as well. While Luther was making noise in what would later become southern Germany, loyal priestly reformers in Rome, the seat of Catholic orthodoxy, were attempting to incorporate similar ideas into Catholic teachings without contradicting them. Thus, the Lutheran turn against Catholicism happened concurrently with repeated, if smaller, turns within Catholicism, ultimately resulting in what has come to be known as the Counter Reformation (or Catholic Reformation, as those in the Catholic church would have it).

Reflecting on such complex events in so many human endeavors, it's easy to see how convoluted and confusing the turns, the objects of them, and the emotions surrounding them can become. In some ways ours is a world of order, from the earth reliably rotating on its axis to the moon's predictable trek across the sky. But it's also a world of mystery as "in the course of human events" we interact with one another and cause history to turn, often in unpredictable ways.

When something turns, whether the direction appears positive or negative, it's natural for us to feel emotions ranging from euphoria to despair. Effective leaders develop an ability to "compartmentalize"; not denying legitimate and appropriate emotions but neither letting their emotions dictate how they will respond to the situation or the myriad other balls they must continually juggle.

Think about the last few turns—large or small—your company has faced. What was your initial reaction? Were you able to separate subject (you) from object (it), and think critically about the implications and options? The bigger the challenge the more difficult this is, but the more vital it becomes to maintain a dispassionate distance. When my company nearly cratered, I spent far too much time staring at the bleary eyes looking back at me in the mirror and beating myself up, which drained away any capability I had to think critically about the problem. It's tough to be creative when you're discouraged.

Things turn. People turn. Things turn people and people turn things. In one sense we are, like the sun, moon, and stars, and like the animals and the atoms of which they're made, simply objects in an ever-revolving universe. In another sense, we're different. We can be aware of turns even as they're happening. We can separate the emotions surrounding them from the factors driving them. We can use judgment, apply wisdom, and distinguish between the turns themselves and the parts we play in them.

Craps players may tell themselves they're simply rolling the dice, but depending on what their larger circumstances are, they may be "rolling the dice" with respect to their lives or the lives of their families. Turning your back on a colleague at work may simply be ending a difficult conversation, or it may result in ending your employment there. Turning over one more page in your research might reveal a clue that unlocks a mystery and changes your fortunes. Objects never turn in isolation, because when something turns, something changes, for everyone and for all time. It's not always dramatic, but it's always true.

The world wouldn't work if every turn required our oversight or supervision. But neither does it work if we resign ourselves to being hapless victims of circumstances. The ability to distinguish between the turns in which we're involved and the roles we play in them is a uniquely human characteristic. The perspective we gain from doing so can empower us to affect both their timing and trajectory. We don't have to just take turns. We can make them.

> ***The Principle of The Object***
> *Distinguishing that which is turning from the turn itself gives us the critical perspective we need to make levelheaded decisions.*

MOMENTS

"If I could turn back time . . ."
Cher

The fall of the Berlin Wall was bound to happen at some point. Built on a lie in the middle of the night, the wall was a tangible representation of the "Iron Curtain" that descended upon Eastern Europe after the end of the Second World War. Propped up by a totalitarian government that was hobbled by a command-and-control economy, it was destined to fall. But when?

No one knew. And nobody could have imagined it would be the result of a bureaucratic snafu.

A little more than two years prior to the wall coming down, President Ronald Reagan stood in front of Berlin's Brandenburg Gate and, over the objections of his own State Department, issued a public challenge to the Soviet Premier: "General Secretary Gorbachev, if you seek peace, if you seek prosperity for the Soviet Union and Eastern Europe, if you seek liberalization, come here to this gate. Mr. Gorbachev, open this gate! Mr. Gorbachev, tear down this wall!"

Though controversial at the time, Reagan's challenge inspired Germans on both sides of the border and increased the pressure Gorbachev felt to loosen the Soviet grip on East Germany. On a mild November afternoon in 1989, government spokesperson Günter Schabowski was instructed to announce at a news conference that East German citizens would soon to be able to cross through the gates with certain restrictions. But he failed to clarify precisely what the restrictions would be, and when a reporter asked when the decision would take effect, Schabowski said, "As far as I know, it takes effect immediately, without delay."

That was all Berliners on both sides of the wall needed to hear. Media immediately began excitedly reporting the news, drawing ever-increasing throngs of people to gather at the gates. Outnumbered and overwhelmed, East German border guards were unsure what to do, and in the confusion, they could find no one who was willing to authorize the use of force. By 11:00 p.m., they had opened the gates and thousands of people pressed through with zero regard for protocol or papers-checking. By midnight the checkpoints were entirely overrun, and Berliners began to climb up on the wall and attack it with picks and sledgehammers. The spontaneous celebration was broadcast live all over the world and, within days, all but symbolic remnants of the wall had been pulverized.

With the fall of the Berlin Wall, a chain of events had been set in motion that no one could stop. Within eleven months, East and West Germany were reunified, effectively marking the end of the Cold War.

What a moment.

It may not have been "The End of History," the title of an essay (and subsequent book) by political scientist Francis Fukuyama written only months before, arguing that Western liberal democracy had triumphed over countries with "ideological pretensions of representing different and higher forms of human society,"[1] but there is no question that it was a major turn in human events.

Why the fall of the Berlin Wall didn't happen a decade earlier, or a decade later, we'll never know. All we know is that at that specific point in time, a fortuitous confluence of circumstances set in motion its demise. Every turn, it seems, has its moment. In strict scientific terms, however, it's more technically correct to say that every turn *is* a moment.

We laypeople tend to think of a "moment" in temporal terms, but to physicists it has a specific, technical meaning. "Moment" is, in fact, a scientific word that describes the measure of the tendency of a force to cause a body to rotate around an axis. The Massachusetts Institute of Technology helpfully describes it via a simple, everyday example:

> Imagine two people pushing on a door at the doorknob from opposite sides. If both of them are pushing with an equal force, then there is a state of equilibrium. If one of them would suddenly jump back from the door, the push of the other person would no longer have any opposition and the door would swing away. The person who was still pushing on the door created a moment.[2]

"The person pushing on the door created a moment." Now that gives us a great deal to work with. We'll address "the person" and "the push" in later chapters (a Cause and a Contest), but isn't it fascinating that the physical moment and temporal moment of a turn are, for all practical purposes, indistinguishable? You can't separate a turn from time.

History is replete with innovations that were introduced before the world was ready. Amazon was not the first online bookseller; Books.com had launched two years prior to Jeff Bezos's first sale. Apple wasn't the first to develop a tablet computer; Cambridge Research and Linus Technologies both introduced one more than two decades earlier. And the first electric car was introduced eighty years before Elon Musk was born. For an innovation to succeed, it must combine a unique mix of utility, affordability, appeal, funding, and yes, timing. Introduce a technology before its time and no one will know how to use it. Wait too long and you may lose the market. Turns and time are inextricably interwoven, not only in chronology, but in duration.

As we've seen, a sprinting swimmer must complete each turn in less than a second to win (though when Sarah Thomas swam the English Channel an astonishing four times in succession, the rules allowed her a ten-minute break at each turn if she remained knee-deep in the water). Electrons whir around the nucleus of an atom at around twenty-eight billion kilometers per second.[3] The earth rotates on its axis every 86,400 seconds and around the sun every 525,600 minutes. The fall of the Berlin Wall happened over the course of several hours, the Cold War lasted multiple decades, and some would say the turn of the Reformation still hasn't ended.

In the early twentieth century, classical music, which had dominated cultural tastes for the previous two hundred years, began to give way to music that was more accessible to a mainstream audience as increasing numbers of people became economically able to afford it. They were more interested in jazz and blues and Tin Pan Alley than Brahms and Bach and Beethoven. Those new musical genres in turn evolved into R&B and Country & Western music, then all of the above into rock-and-roll. This series of musical moments all happened within roughly a fifty-year period, following which continued evolutions have emerged on a decade-by-decade basis.

In part driven by this continuous evolution of genres, robust sales of cassettes and compact discs (plus a handful of vinyl albums favored by die-hard audiophiles) led music industry revenues to reach some $21.5 billion a year around the turn of the twenty-first century. But when music went digital with the advent of Napster, followed by iTunes, then Spotify and Pandora, sales of recordings in physical format plummeted to less than $7 billion a year. Suddenly, and seemingly without warning, new releases no longer translated into rising revenues, and for more than a decade both artists and music companies reeled. To make up the difference, they turned from record sales to live concerts, but were then hit with a global pandemic that shut down public gatherings of any kind. It was a series of turns that knocked the industry on its ear.[4]

As the late decades of the twentieth century in the music industry demonstrated, prior to a turn there is some sort of equilibrium. Balance. Stability. Predictability. Like when you're driving across flat, barren terrain with nothing to look at but white lines as far as the eye can see. As boring as that can be, there's something comfortable about it. Unrisky. Safe. It's the perfect moment to put on the cruise control. But not to quit paying attention; sooner or later, there will come a moment when you're faced with a turn.

Roadway engineers have done such a fantastic job preparing turns for us that we rarely have to think about them. Professor Findley says that a curve has one job, simply to provide a smooth transition between two tangents, which we might call straightaways. That's an interesting way of thinking about it.

Smooth transitions are always better than the alternative. In an automobile, of course, they're a function of many variables. There's the road, for one—its material, temperature, width, crown, number of lanes, age, markings, guardrails, signage, and more. There's the curve itself—its radius, elevation, length, line of sight, obstructions, vehicular traffic, and more. There's the car—its weight, speed, suspension, windshield, wipers (gotta factor in rain or snow), brakes, tires, and more. And there's the driver, with a whole host of individual variables including not only his or her height, eyesight, hearing, and reflexes, but also state of mind, attention span, appetite for risk, and a variety of potential distractions, from listening to loud music to getting lost in an audiobook, chatting with a friend on the phone, or scolding kids in the back seat.

Fortunately, automotive engineers have made cars ever safer, and roadway engineers like Dr. Findley have accounted for as many of the physical variables as possible. They make the radius of a turn as wide as feasible. They can create banks in the turns and carefully calculate how vehicles can make a smooth transition from the normal crown of a roadway through each curve and back. They consider the "visual noise" of such variables as lights, buildings, and billboards surrounding the roadway.

They even factor in things like "perception-reaction time" (PRT), which is the time it takes a typical driver to recognize an unexpected obstacle or road condition, and "maneuver time" (MT), the time it takes to complete the resulting maneuver safely. PRT and MT are factors that go into calculating "decision sight distance," which is the length of roadway an average driver requires to detect an unexpected hazard in a visually cluttered environment, recognize the hazard's threat potential, adjust the vehicle's speed and path, and safely maneuver around the obstacle and back to equilibrium.[5] All of this is difficult enough to do on straightaways; it's even more complex in turns.

Thank God for roadway engineers. As long as drivers approach curves with a reasonable expectation of the proper timing of the turn, most of which feature prominently posted speed limit signs, they'll neither fly off the curve by going too fast or get rear-ended by going too slow. And if a deer or a dog should suddenly appear in the middle of the road, they ought to be able to get around it safely.

Not every turn in business is so predictable, however. In fact, most are not. Which is why it's important to cultivate the ability to see turns coming, or at least to recognize them as soon as they appear on the horizon. The more time we have to prepare for turns, the more assuredly we'll be able to get through them in one piece. Especially when they're harrowing.

The Civil War officially began on April 12, 1861, when the Confederate Army attacked Fort Sumter near Charleston, South Carolina. While the where and when of the attack had been uncertain, the nation, and its new president, had sensed that the moment was imminent. "With the two-party political system gone, there was no way to mediate disputes," says Derek Frisby. "There was no way to compromise. So, the momentum was toward war." The armed conflict ended April 9, 1865, with Lee's surrender at Appomattox. In one sense, the Civil War "moment" was that specific four-year period.

The hostilities themselves, however, were bookended by two moments of historical irony. The first happened in 1861, just prior to the war, when President Lincoln was sworn in by Supreme Court justice Roger Taney, the author of the Dred Scott decision which ruled that people of African descent weren't citizens and thus had no right to sue in federal court, and that slave owners' rights were protected by the Fifth Amendment because slaves were their legal property.[6] The second was a near-miss that occurred four years later; in the epilogue to his epic recounting of the Civil War, *Battle Cry of Freedom*, James McPherson points out that, "If Lincoln had been defeated for re-election in 1864, as he anticipated in August, history might record [Jefferson] Davis as the great war leader and Lincoln as an also-ran."[7] It's remarkable on what moments history can turn.

While the length of the Civil War can be clearly demarcated, the "moment" that the war began could forever be debated. The Northern states had been the first slaveholding governments in the world to abolish slavery, and the U.S. was the first nation in the world to begin actively suppressing the slave trade (though Great Britain was the first to abolish it).[8] That only added to the tensions that had been mounting for decades between North and South, mollified and/or exacerbated by moments such as the Missouri Compromise and the Kansas–Nebraska Act. The original question of slavery had been left to future generations by the nation's Founding Fathers and punted by successive presidents. Beyond that, the institution of slavery had been around since time immemorial, with the abolition of the slave trade and ultimately slavery itself in the British Commonwealth all factoring into the long turning of the tide against one of humanity's most shameful practices.

And the end of the Civil War "moment" is also debatable. Lee's surrender on April 9, 1865, meant no more official clashes on the battlefield, but it did not result in the end of hostilities. Juneteenth is celebrated today because it wasn't until June 19 of that year that slaves in Texas were informed by General Gordon Granger that "in accordance with a Proclamation from the Executive of the United States, all slaves are free."[9]

Beyond that, the era of Reconstruction was anything but smooth. Significant progress was made in the years following the war—in 1865 the Thirteenth Amendment outlawed slavery, three years later the Fourteenth Amendment extended citizenship and equal protection under the law to anyone born in the United States, and two years after that the Fifteenth Amendment granted all men the right to vote. But one of the implications of ending the centuries-old institution of slavery was a turn whose complexities nobody could fully comprehend.

In 1877, federal troops were officially removed from the Southern states, kneecapping the effort to add justice in peace to victory in war. "Too tired of trying to enforce Reconstruction laws," says Professor Frisby, "they just gave up." That paved the way for the Jim Crow era separating whites from "persons of color" in places like schools, restaurants, and theaters, and on public transportation. The Jim Crow moment continued for nearly a century until civil rights legislation in the 1960s put an end to official segregation. Even then, the work was not complete.

So how should we best characterize the "moment" that was the Civil War? Is it as simple as the four years between 1861 and 1865? Is it more accurate to date it from 1788, when the U.S. Constitution was ratified, to 1964 and the passage of the Civil Rights Act? Or was the bloody mid-nineteenth-century conflict in which 750,000 Americans lost their lives the apex of a very long turn from an ancient and inhumane practice to today's unquestioned understanding (at least in the West) that all men are created equal? Viewing it through the lens of any of the three moments—or others—enables us to consider different perspectives.

The same can be said of turns in business. Something we believe is correct in the moment could result in regret down the road. Something that causes distress today might turn out to be a blessing tomorrow. My firm once worked with a well-known landscaping company that specialized in making all things green—lush lawns, thriving gardens, rich flowerbeds, bushy trees. Then came what scientists call a two-decade (and counting) "megadrought" across the Western United States, spawning both a cultural and practical trend toward landscaping that requires no more water than what's ambiently available. Naturally, this turn put a dent in the prospects of the landscaping company, and its ownership faced a growing crisis.

Or opportunity. We recognized that native landscaping was a new and little-understood concept to many homeowners, many of whom associated it only with a narrow, rocks-and-cactus slice known as "xeriscaping." We thought the time might be just right to convert the company's water-soaked acres of nurseries into a showcase of beautiful native landscaping displays. Just as walking through an IKEA store enables customers to see a variety of furniture and accessory combinations laid out in a series of real-world settings, we believed that homeowners who were concerned enough about the environment to want to replace their lawns would love the idea of exploring a variety of native landscape options.

We even suspected that this approach would generate additional revenue opportunities, as the company could sell not only the materials for and installation of new outdoor environments but a host of accessories as well. Alas, rather than recognizing that this new model might be a turn whose time had come, ownership made a change-resistant, reflexive decision to try and ride out the drought. The company didn't make it.

Sometimes our reflexes are all we have; if two cars collide in front of you, there may be no choice but to swerve. Short of life-and-death situations, however, thoughtful reflection is usually wise, considering not only the anticipated but also possible unintended consequences of a turn. Just as chess masters consider multiple scenarios that might unfold prior to moving their bishop or rook, taking a deep breath and a long look is usually a good idea.

Instead, we often act as if we're heroic protagonists in a Hollywood blockbuster, in which the more spine-tingling the action the more compelling the scene. Directors and screenwriters are masters of the dramatic moment, that turn in a tale that indicates to the audience that something is changing, and the characters will never be the same.

In *It's a Wonderful Life*, Frank Capra's optimistic, post-WWII morality tale, there's a moment when George Bailey, played by a dapper Jimmy Stewart (who in real life had recently returned from the war), shares one end of an old-fashioned telephone with Mary Hatch, played by the lovely Donna Reed. On the other end of the line was Mary's sometimes-suitor, Sam Wainwright, droning on about plastics and investments and what George should do with his money. Then comes the moment when George, realizing that he's listening less to Sam than to his wildly beating heart, drops the phone, takes Mary in his arms, confesses his feelings, and surrenders to his destiny. It's one of the most romantic moments in film.

In *The Wizard of Oz,* the dramatic turn is when Dorothy realizes that there is no Wizard, only a man behind the curtain. In *The Empire Strikes Back* it's when Darth Vader tells Luke Skywalker, "I am your father." In *You've Got Mail* it's when "Shopgirl" Meg Ryan finally realizes that "NY152" Tom Hanks is the online partner with whom she has been corresponding and falling in love. And in *The Lord of the Rings* trilogy there are several dramatic turns, from when Gandalf took on the Balrog in *The Fellowship of the Ring* ("You shall not pass!") to the better-late-than-never arrival of the Rohirrim to save Minas

Tirith in *The Return of the King*, to Aragorn's daring call to arms at the Black Gate of Mordor ("It is not this day!"). "You had me at hello" is also a pretty good moment at the end of *Jerry Maguire*—who, let's not forget, became a successful first mover by anticipating an innovative turn in his industry.

The reason a dramatic moment works in story better than real life again mirrors physics. In the world of objects, a moment (turn) is a series of vectors, which are scientifically defined as having two characteristics, magnitude and direction—think of a flying arrow. Vectors are always straight, which means a turn is really a continuous series of vectors adjacent to one another, each having a slightly different direction.

Picture going for a walk and making a gradual, ninety-degree leftward turn. By simply adjusting each foot to fall one degree farther to the left with every progressive step, in ninety steps you will have turned ninety degrees along ninety different vectors. Complete the turn and you complete a moment. In the movies, all the changing vectors can be sped up, as days, weeks, and sometimes years are compressed into mere minutes. In real life, we have to deal with each vector as it comes.

Why the science? Because as much as we believe our companies are "walking straight," the reality is that they're continually changing direction. The vector that is each day flows so smoothly into the next that we don't always realize we're turning—or that events are turning around us. If you've ever tried to walk a straight line on the beach, build a cinderblock wall, or lay tile, you know it's impossible to do so without using some sort of plumb line to keep you from zigzagging all over the place. Each minor change in direction is compounded by the ones before it.

Like the Civil War, the Reformation "moment" had many diverse vectors and can be characterized by as many different time frames as there are Reformation scholars. Was it 1517 to 1525, the first few high stakes years after Luther, *contra mundum*, performed his solo act of defiance? Or is it better thought of as the years 1400 to 1750, a period *The Oxford Handbook of the Protestant Reformations* calls the "long Reformation" during which centuries of virtual stasis slowly gave way to enlightened thinking and the dawn of the Scientific Revolution? Did it begin in the days of the early church to which reformers hearkened back and continue to the Second Great Awakening of the early nineteenth century? Or could it be understood as a slow yet unceasing turn from the original Abrahamic covenant to the present day, the apex of which was the birth of Christ? Regardless of whether one demarcates BC from AD or BCE from CE, we nod to that turning point in history every time we date a letter or fill out an expense report.

Any of these notions regarding the Reformation "moment" can be instructive, especially given the perspective of time. Alec Ryrie describes the Reformation as a composite event that can only be seen by framing it after the fact. "Sixteenth- and seventeenth-century English people knew that they were living through an age of religious upheaval," he says, "but they did not know that it was 'the English Reformation', any more than the soldiers at the battle of Agincourt knew that they were fighting in 'the Hundred Years' War.'"[10]

From our position in the present, it's easy to see some of the more notable vectors of any historical turn. "There's a foreshortening as we look backwards," says Rutgers's Tia Kolbaba. "Well, that only took two centuries." Still, as historian Megan Armstrong puts it, "There's something about the Reformation itself as a moment of religious change that was fracturing in a way that overshadowed everything else for a period of time."[11]

Up until the early 1500s, things had remained unchanged for hundreds of years. The Catholic Church, the feudal economy, the cycles of the seasons, and the rhythms of life continued each day much as they had in the past. But in the period just prior to the birth of Luther, things began to destabilize—a lot.

There was the continuing fallout from the Little Ice Age, a period of global cooling caused by the effects of a series of big volcanic eruptions, which resulted in widespread crop failure, fish migration, famine, and population decline. Urbanization had been expanding in Europe, along with associated economic integration. Nationalism was starting to arise in places like England, France, and Spain, pulling them away from Rome and unified Christendom.

It was The Age of Discovery—of Galileo and Copernicus and Columbus and the questioning of the previously unquestionable. Art was flourishing as never before. In 1503, as Michelangelo was laboring over what would become the world's most famous sculpture, *David*, less than a mile away Leonardo da Vinci was painting the *Mona Lisa*. "With the benefit of considerable hindsight, one can see that the common factor between them, which is unique to the West, was the maturing appreciation for artistic creativity as the human analogue of divine creativity," says Victoria Coates, author of *David's Sling: A History of Democracy in Ten Works of Art*. "Since antiquity," she says, "artists had been considered manual laborers who functioned as physical tools that manifested the vision of their patrons. That had started to change in the early Renaissance, famously with Dante's assertion in the *Inferno* that art, which imitates nature, imitates the creation of God."[12]

Literacy was spreading for the first time, accelerated by the invention of the printing press in 1436. It may have been this development that was most consequential. Professor and theologian Carl Trueman underscores just how momentous it was to the nascent Protestant movement: "The church finally starts to get access to whole texts of [early church father] Augustine. Luther emerges out of Wittenberg out of a group of academics who are reading Augustine and beginning to discover that certain of the teachings they've received from their late Medieval masters on the issue of grace do not conform with what Augustine himself was teaching about grace."[13]

The printing press not only played a key role in Luther's revival; it was critical to his survival. "It's impossible to think of Luther surviving in a way that Jan Hus couldn't without the printing press," says John Craig, professor at Simon Fraser University and author of two books on the Reformation. "Luther was able, through printers and publishers who were sympathetic to his views, to get out these smart, punchy attacks on papal authority. The printing press is absolutely crucial in shaping people's ideas and allowing him space to survive."[14]

Tia Kolbaba is of similar mind. "There are two things to me that make the Reformation succeed where, say, Jan Hus didn't, and ended up burned at the stake. One of them is that Luther can get the word out [via the printing press]. The other is the political backing that he and Calvin and Melanchthon and Zwingli had. The powers that be that should have been putting down this heresy decided to throw in with the heresy instead. Every foundation there is was being challenged."[15]

Indeed, Luther's books were on sale in Oxford as early as 1520,[16] and over the course of the rest of his life he published 1,465 pamphlets, averaging about one every three weeks. Other pro-Luther authors added some eight hundred tracts, while his detractors published only three hundred—and mostly in

Latin, whereas Luther wrote in German, the language of the commoner.[17] He may have been the inspiration for the tongue-in-cheek warning to politicians about the press, "Never pick a fight with someone who buys their ink in barrels."

It is remarkable to consider the impact on history of the technological innovation of movable type. When Johannes Gutenberg invented the printing press in the mid-1400s, he seemed to know he was on to something big, as evidenced by the secrecy with which he perfected his machine. But he couldn't have anticipated how his innovation would change the course of history. Without the printing press, Luther may have become a footnote in history. Which may have meant no Reformation, no end to slavery, no America, and certainly not your company or mine (perhaps not even you or me). But I'm getting ahead of myself.

The moment of the Reformation had been set in motion by a convergence of events, from the rise of cities to the rapid dissemination of ideas. Yet there was something about the specific moment of October 31, 1517, when Luther nailed his ninety-five theses to the Wittenberg Church door, that caused the dam to break. "Within weeks," says Carl Trueman, "the treatise has been translated and is being spread as a pamphlet across electoral Saxony . . . Luther said more radical things a month before and nobody cared. . . . It's this that triggers the explosion of the Reformation."[18]

Could Luther have known this? Highly unlikely. In fact, it's instructive to consider exactly what may have been going through his mind at the time. He may have thought, motivated by his sincere desire to improve the church, not attack it, that he would be welcomed as a reformer. He may have expected, based on the fate of those who had challenged the authority of the church before him, that he would be burned at the stake. Perhaps, based on what we know about Luther's personality, he may have feared being ignored altogether. What Luther did know, however, was that this was his moment. Circumstances had brought him to a mental and moral crossroads, and he knew he had to act.

Despite our being half a world—and half a millennium—away from Luther, we can relate. Most of the turns we face, or initiate, are not matters of life and death—or so we assume. But our ability to recognize and embrace these moments helps ensure that we will neither miss them nor mess them up. It requires us to remain alert to all that is going on around, and inside, us.

The biggest corporation my firm has consulted is a *Fortune 100* manufacturer with operations around the world. The company's "moment" had lasted for more than a century by the time our paths crossed. Having recently undertaken a significant evolution of its business model, it began to dawn on leadership that with each passing day, what the brand was known for in the marketplace fit less well with what it was becoming, and—critically—its tens of thousands of employees could soon be facing an unanticipated identity crisis. It became increasingly clear to them that a worldwide rebranding effort was in order, enhancing their ability to manage the turn before anybody got nauseous. They recognized the need only because they had been paying attention to the moment.

Alec Ryrie sums up how the convergence of factors that uniquely came together during the early 1500s accelerated the Reformation, which, to that point, had begun only in fits and starts: "The slow spread of literacy, accelerated by the development of printing in the mid-fifteenth century, symbolized a change in how lay Christians related to their Church. No longer simply the passive consumers of its sacramental services and the subjects of its prayers, they were participating."[19] He goes on to describe the spread of the movement in terms a global corporation might find familiar: "Luther's seeds were scattered [in England] as they were everywhere. Merchants plying the North Sea routes were vectors for the new ideas."[20]

Between both the Protestant and Catholic Reformations, the process of change in the church has arguably never ended, and likely never will, this side of heaven. And like virtually all turns, once it was set in motion, it set other things in motion, perhaps most notably the scientific foundation for ongoing advances in technology that we've come to expect today.

In the sixteenth and seventeenth centuries, the term *laws of nature* began to be used to describe observable scientific regularities in the writings of religious "natural philosophers" such as Francis Bacon, now known as the father of empiricism; René Descartes, who came to the famous philosophical conclusion "I think, therefore I am"; and Isaac Newton, the first scientist to be knighted and whom astrophysicist Neil DeGrasse Tyson called "the millennium's most brilliant and influential person."[21]

The post-Reformation worldview of these men led them away from describing nature through the Aristotelian lens of axioms—self-evident first principles for which no proof is required—and toward empirical observation, documentation, and mathematics. It was the beginning of the Scientific Revolution and another sweeping moment of change. As Stephen C. Meyer, who earned his Cambridge PhD in the philosophy of science, put it, "Only a few centuries after Newton characterized the universal law of gravity, human beings harnessed this knowledge to put men on the moon."[22]

That's no coincidence. Today we know that the moon's orbit affects tides on earth through its gravitational pull. Essentially, the oceans that face the moon bulge toward it, a phenomenon we know as high tide. Because the ocean is liquid, other points on earth experience low tide at the same time. As the earth spins, high and low tide move around the globe every twenty-four hours, resulting in two high tides and two low tides each day. Since the moon orbits the earth every twenty-seven days, high and low tide times vary slightly, but they are totally predictable. We have Isaac Newton's original insight to thank for that.

Without Newton there may have been no Einstein, a German physicist of Jewish descent who immigrated to the United States during the rise of Adolf Hitler. In 1939, Einstein wrote a letter to President Franklin Roosevelt warning that the Nazis were working on a terrifying new weapon: an atomic bomb. Shortly after the Japanese attacked Pearl Harbor in December 1941, Roosevelt launched the Manhattan Project, which would ultimately lead to the development, testing, and first use of the bomb in August 1945. It was a moment that changed weaponry, war, and energy forever, not to mention the global balance of power, ending the war in Asia and making the United States the twentieth century's lone superpower.

But not for long. Just four years later, the Soviet Union tested its first nuclear weapon. And less than a decade after that, the Soviets launched Sputnik, the first artificial earth satellite, which sent shock waves through the free world and led President John F. Kennedy to call for the U.S. to be the first country to put a man on the moon. The space race began at that moment.

In economics, as in science and religion and the events of our lives, one moment leads to another in an endless series of turns. The year 1776 was notable not only for the signing of the Declaration of Independence; it was also the year Adam Smith's *An Inquiry into the Nature and Causes of the Wealth of Nations* was first published. The economic moment that was feudalism had enjoyed a good, thousand-year run between the fifth and fifteenth centuries, but as the stability of the Middle Ages gave way to questioning old assumptions and the advent of the scientific method, concepts such as free trade, innovation, and entrepreneurialism began to gain currency. Smith was the first to offer an explanation as to why.

Perhaps because it had originated in Britain, the Industrial Revolution had an underappreciated impact on the Civil War. The Northern United States was, in the late eighteenth century, arguably the world's most entrepreneurial region, buzzing with innovation, invention, and investment in public education—in short, industrialization. The South at that time remained a more agrarian society based on forced labor, and the cultural differences between North and South became ever more pronounced. At the beginning of the nineteenth century there was a sense that slavery may have been a fading force, considering what William Wilberforce had accomplished in Great Britain along with the elimination of the slave trade in the U.S. Then came the invention of the cotton gin, which in an odd turn of history enabled the slave states to become much more productive.

Patented only two years before Smith wrote *The Wealth of Nations*, the cotton gin ("gin" being short for "engine") made it easier for cotton growers to remove seeds, which theoretically would reduce the need for labor—slave or free. Inventor Eli Whitney believed it would both hasten the end of slavery and make him rich. Alas, neither was the case. U.S. patent laws were not sufficient to protect him from those who stole his idea, and the machine made cotton growing so much more profitable that it actually increased demand of plantation owners for land and labor.

Thus, just as slavery's moment appeared to be ending, the Industrial Revolution gave it a shot in the arm, further straining ties between North and South. "So," says Derek Frisby, "you have this extraordinary bifurcation of the United States into two ultimately antagonistic economies," increasing the sense of "otherness" and the appeal of secession. In another historical irony, however, the credibility Whitney earned as an inventor helped him win a contract with the federal government to mass-produce muskets based on the new idea of interchangeable parts, which would contribute to the North's industrial advantage in the Civil War.

What's so fascinating and instructive about moments like these is that they can be viewed up close as a sequence of directly related events or through the broader lens of sweeping historical trends. From an economic standpoint, slavery as practiced in the ancient empires had largely given way to feudalism hundreds of years earlier. Feudalism in turn gave way to industrialism, temporarily fortifying slavery, which has since been superseded by the information economy. Through it all, individual actors made individual decisions in specific local contexts, without appreciating how one turn affects another in their own lives, let alone in the broader sweep of history.

Joel Mokyr, professor of economics at Northwestern University, says, "In economic history much of the change that matters is quiet, underneath the surface, and the effects don't show up until a generation later." He notes that those who were active in the early days of the Industrial Revolution probably didn't realize it and would have no concept that continuous innovation and productivity growth were to become the new normal. "Most of the macroeconomic effects do not show up in the aggregative statistics, such as they are, until many decades after the great inventions," he says.[23]

It continues in today's information economy. Over the course of more than one hundred years, information age pioneer IBM has survived through several challenging moments. The organization's beginnings date back to 1911 when a businessman named Charles Flint merged three small technology companies: one that made scales, one that made rudimentary tabulating machines, and one that made time clocks for factory workers. He unimaginatively called it the Computing-Tabulating-Recording-Company, or C-T-R. A few years later, Thomas J. Watson joined the company as general manager and, in 1924, wisely changed its name to International Business Machines.

IBM's first moment of crisis was the recession of 1920–21, during which its revenue declined by almost 35 percent. Ten years later came the Great Depression and three consecutive years of flat or declining sales. The significant industrial needs brought on by World War II resulted in several years of growth, but the company's fortunes took another turn shortly after the end of the war. Following that, IBM rode the wave of the postwar years with a four-decade-plus tear of uninterrupted growth.

In his book *Making the World Better: The Ideas That Shaped a Century and a Company*, Kevin Maney says, "Watson fashioned C-T-R into a very different sort of company from those that surrounded him. He realized that his company's counting and calculating devices could help those railroads, steel companies, manufacturers and merchants manage their data. He saw that in the new century, a company's most valuable assets would be the information it amassed, the knowledge it created and the ideas of its employees—intellectual capital rather than money, muscle, or raw material."[24] You might say Watson recognized the moment.

By 1955 Watson's son Thomas Jr. had assumed the mantle of leadership from his father and was featured on the cover of *Time* magazine as the star of its cover story, "The Brain Builders." The other star of the story was IBM's Model 702 Electronic Data Processing Machine, which the article described as "the giant brain." It could perform 7,200 logical operations per second, equivalent to the capabilities of 25,000 mathematicians.[25] Though merely a tiny fraction of today's computing power, at that time it was like nothing the world had ever seen.

Then IBM ran into a series of challenging turns. First was the recession of the early 1990s, which resulted in a mild dip in revenues. Ten years later came the dot-com bust, followed by the 9/11 economic slowdown. Then arch-rival Hewlett-Packard purchased Compaq to form a more formidable foe, and due to technological advances, prices for computer processing power began tumbling at a rate of 50 percent per year. Ten years later came the financial crisis and the Great Recession, during which time the global financial system was in a state of shock and many of IBM's customers struggled to ride out the storm. Following that was the rise of cloud computing and stiff competition from Google, Microsoft, and Amazon Web Services, companies that were nimbler than IBM and able to grab a commanding market share.

None of these moments were of IBM's own making, nor were they things the company could have anticipated. Its biggest new competitor, however, did anticipate the most recent change. In fact, it created much of it. When Jeff Bezos took Amazon public just two years after the company's founding, he repeatedly made clear to his shareholders that growth was more important than dividends. The company lost hundreds of millions of dollars until it turned its first annual profit six years later, but that was all part of the plan. In fact, the year Amazon passed the $5 billion revenue mark, it was about the same size as RadioShack, which at its peak had a store within five miles of every American. In the years that followed, Amazon swallowed up RadioShack's market share like an alligator devouring a turtle.

Bezos's strategy was to seize the early internet moment and establish a beachhead that no competitor could challenge, and he put his money where his mouth was. Investors who got in early, and stayed in, enjoyed the fruits of his vision and patience.

Netflix followed a similar path, willing to lose money for its first six years and even spurning an early offer from Amazon to buy the company. But soon after it became profitable, Netflix lost its patience and in so doing created its own painful turn of events. Wanting to separate customers of its nascent streaming service from those who ordered DVDs by mail, the company decided to raise its prices and assign many of its subscribers to a new brand, Qwikster, without their consent. Eight hundred thousand customers and almost 80 percent of Netflix's market value disappeared in a single quarter, and the company immediately reversed course.

Mastering the moment of a turn is no picnic, as IBM, Netflix, and Sundt all learned. Doug Pruitt became president of Sundt during the month of August, shortly before the company closed its books in September, revealing that it had experienced its worst financial year in its history. About that moment he says,

> What I quickly discovered was that Sundt was losing millions of dollars. I also learned that the company had a long list of construction claims and litigation. I started digging into finances at the operating level and realized what a dysfunctional, financially sick organization Sundt had

> become. I saw groups and divisions that hadn't been consistently profitable for ten years. Why hadn't these groups been shut down? How did it get this bad? What had I become president of? I have always enjoyed a challenge. Becoming president of a company was something I aspired to, but this was not exactly what I had dreamed of.[26]

At the very time he should have been most gratified at having been elevated to the top, he said, "I realized I'd been given the helm of a sinking ship." In the years leading up to that time he had been proud to watch the company where he had spent his entire career build tremendously complex projects, not realizing that it was losing money hand over fist doing so. "I think we'd have gone broke if somebody didn't stand up and say, 'this is stupid.' The turn for me came when I finally had a chance to do something about it."

Pruitt recognized the moment of truth Sundt was facing and wasted no time. He sold non-performing assets to help offset the losses and spent three years "grabbing the wheel to avoid the crash." Those first thirty-six months were the most critical, but as is typical of turnarounds, the problems had begun years earlier and would reverberate for years to come.

Pruitt is not the first CEO to have to deal with turnaround issues, nor was Sundt the only company to struggle with wrenching change. Since the Industrial Age began, the cycle of disruption–acceleration–maturation–saturation–commoditization has been speeding up. In our grandparents' day it was more difficult to see because the cycle moved more slowly than the average person's career span; it's why people often had one job for life. But like the hands of a clock, the wheels of change were always turning, if imperceptibly.

Baby Boomers were told that they should prepare themselves to have more than one career, and today we counsel our young people to become continuous, lifelong learners and remain flexible and resilient, knowing their career arcs may turn in a variety of directions.

We've all lived this reality. It's quaint to think of having a job for life, but in reality, we're all continually evaluating whether, and when, it may be time to move on. Ours is an age of both instability and opportunity, and in that respect we face more frequent decisions than our forebears in terms of what to do with our lives. That is a privilege, to be sure, but also a burden. Professionally speaking, we must continually discern the meaning of the moments in which we find ourselves.

It's as true for organizations as it is for individuals. Over the past half-century, the average tenure of a company in the S&P 500 has decreased from sixty-five years to less than ten. Fewer than 10 percent of *Fortune 500* companies have been on that list since the middle of the last century. And many of the companies that could afford expensive Super Bowl ads during Tom Brady's first appearance in the game were out of business before his last one.

Sometimes we know exactly when our moment is about to happen, like when a quarterback gets the ball with two minutes left in the game. Sometimes we seize the moment as it unfolds, like an entrepreneur quitting a secure job to bring a new software idea to life. And sometimes we don't see a turn coming at all, like an unanticipated layoff we never could have predicted. We can't always choose the timing of our turns, but the sooner we can recognize them, the better.

The lesson of the moment is simply this: be in it. Turns are difficult enough to navigate when you're paying attention and engaged; the alternative is to run off (or get run off) the road. Change, as a rule, makes everything feel faster; a basketball careening off the rim causes momentary chaos, as does an Olympic skier briefly becoming airborne as she rounds the gates of the giant slalom. It's important to stay calm, neither rushing nor delaying your reaction.

That's not easy to do, because time feels different in turns. Think of a record spinning on a turntable. As counterintuitive as it sounds, a point on the outside edge of the disc must move significantly faster than one on the inside if it is to complete a 360-degree rotation in the same amount of time. Similarly, the outside wheels on a turning car must rotate faster than those on the inside. In fact, science tells us that if you lock an object into a single turning radius it will continually pick up speed. That gets to death-by-whirlpool territory fast.

Golfers can take all the time they need to examine the break in the green before their putt. Runners can leisurely walk the track, clearing it of debris before their race. Scientists can research the literature and the state of the art in their specialty before committing to their next research initiative. In business we can plan ahead, but often we must take turns as they come, and that's where experience, alertness, and instinct pay off.

Malcolm Gladwell, author of *Blink: The Power of Thinking Without Thinking*, says, "On straightforward choices, deliberate analysis is best. When questions of analysis and personal choice start to get complicated—when we have to juggle many different variables—then our unconscious thought processes may be superior."[27] Fine-tuning that mental muscle memory will pay dividends down the road—as long as we don't succumb to our emotions as discussed in the previous chapter.

How do we know whether we've got the inside track or are on the outside edge of a turn? How can we tell what degree of turn we're entering? How can we gauge all the forces at work in a turn when there isn't a thoughtful engineer who has paved the way or helpful signs to guide us through? We must keep our senses keen, our gaze alert, and our minds open. It's remarkable how well drivers can navigate even unfamiliar winding roads based on instinct, sensory cues, and the muscle memory of having done so thousands of times. The same can apply to many of the moments we face in business, if we recognize what's happening.

Lincoln couldn't predict the outcome of any battle before it happened. Luther didn't know he would avoid martyrdom, unlike many of those before who had shared his convictions. Newton could not have foreseen that his insight about gravity would one day help put a man on the moon. Günter Schabowski had no idea that his bungled news conference would lead to the effacement of an empire.

None of us can know what the outcome of the turns we face will be. But it's not only what happens today that's relevant, it's what happened yesterday, and the day before. And what will happen tomorrow. Should someone in the music industry have anticipated what impact its move to digital would have on physical sales? Perhaps. Should the owners of the nursery have taken the ramifications of a megadrought more seriously? Probably. But it's easy to play Monday-morning quarterback regarding decisions someone else has made. More difficult is ensuring that we understand the moment in which we find our own companies.

Set aside some time to consider what happened in your industry in the last year and how it relates to what you anticipate will happen in the coming year. Then consider what happened in the past five years and how it relates to what might happen in the next five. Do the same with the past and next decade (or two) and see if you can spot long-term turns you may be in the midst of. If they're slow and smooth, the vectors might be shifting under your feet without your realizing it, and you might be facing the equivalent of music digitization or a megadrought that future generations will regret you didn't spot. Or perhaps you may be able to initiate a turn that will catch your competitors off guard and keep you ahead of the curve.

The only thing you must not do is stand still, or assume the world is standing still. Each turn will ultimately be judged good or bad based on whether and to what extent you recognize, and seize, its moment. Economist George Gilder says, "The investor who never acts until the statistics affirm his choice, the athlete or politician who fails to make his move until too late, the businessman who waits until the market is proven—all are doomed to mediocrity by their trust in spurious rationality and their failures of faith."[28]

Some turns happen over millennia (tectonic shifts, human migrations). Some over centuries (religious reforms, the rise and fall of civilizations). Some turns take decades to complete (political cycles) and others, years (economic cycles). The life span of some insects lasts less than a day, and the latest science suggests the universe began in an instant. There's no telling when a turn will arise, or how long it will last. The best we can do is sense the moment and be *in* it.

> ***The Principle of The Moment***
> *Every turn has its time. Cultivating the ability to recognize the moment makes us better able to seize it and shape it.*

CAUSES

"Turn me loose."
Loverboy

It had been fifty-eight years since the Chicago Cubs played in a World Series, and ninety-five years since they'd won it—way back when Teddy Roosevelt was president.

Then came the 2003 National League Championship Series in which a stacked Cubs team was leading the Florida Marlins three games to two and had a 3–0 lead in the eighth inning of game six at Wrigley Field. The long-suffering Cubs were just five outs away from the World Series when Marlins second baseman Luis Castillo hit a long fly ball in the direction of Cubs outfielder Moises Alou. Alou, a four-time all-star at that point (he would go on to make a total of six all-star appearances), chased it to the left field wall and leapt to make what would have been an easy catch. "There's no doubt in my mind that I would've caught the ball," he later said.[1] But the catch wasn't to be.

A loyal Cubs fan, doing what fans do when a foul ball comes their way, reached out to make the catch himself, deflecting it into the stands and away from Alou's glove. The Cubs went on to give up eight runs that inning, lose the game, lose the

National League pennant, and once again watch the World Series from home.

Was that single bungled play the cause of the Cubs squandering their shot at glory for the fifty-ninth straight year? It's hard to believe that it could have been. But there was a sense to those who watched it at the time that this one moment changed everything.

Causes of turns, like moments, can be complicated. Many longtime Chicagoans were convinced that fan interference wasn't the root of the Cubs' heartbreaking loss but simply that year's manifestation of "The Curse of the Billy Goat," a local legend that dated back to the 1945 World Series and the owner of the Billy Goat Tavern, William Sianis. Incensed when he wasn't allowed to keep his pet goat (for whom he had purchased a box seat) in the grandstand, Sianis proclaimed, "Them Cubs, they ain't gonna win no more."[2] Sure enough, the team went on to lose that series and, for the next half-century, the Curse of the Billy Goat seemed to be as good an explanation as any for the Cubs' woes.

The fan who interfered with Alou's catch may have played a role in the team's '03 NLCS collapse, but only a small one. After all, to lose the series the Cubs were outplayed in a variety of ways over the subsequent nineteen-and-a-half innings. Who knows what was going through the players' minds about the team's haunted past that may have influenced their play? Whatever the case, it's a great story with an ultimately happy ending: the Cubs broke the curse in 2016 and were kind enough to give the interfering fan from thirteen years prior his own World Series ring. That's the stuff of which movies are made.

It's also the stuff of which ads are made. One way to think about advertisements is that they're like mini movies that tell a story with a purpose: to get the viewer to take some sort of action. But marketers struggle to figure out exactly how much credit to give each ad, a challenge they refer to as "the attribution problem." It arises every time companies attempt to determine which of their ads cause which effects.

Say it's a Saturday and I have decided to go car shopping. Before I leave the house, I see an ad on my phone for the newest Mercedes-Benz model in which I'm already interested, so I click on it to learn more. If I end up buying the car, should that ad get the credit?

The short answer is no. My desire for a Mercedes has been built up over a lifetime of being exposed to the company's ads—not to mention its cars on the street, the brand's appearances in movies and television shows, and the test drive I took that morning. To credit a single click with such a substantial purchase would be silly, but the data does show that one ad, and my interaction with it, as most proximate to my purchase. It played some role in my decision, but what, exactly? That's a question that can never fully be answered.

This attribution problem affects every category of advertising and gets even more difficult to discern when marketers are trying to account for advertising's effects on inexpensive, oft-purchased items such as soft drinks, shoes, and other goods consumers can buy directly online by clicking a link. Proximate causes are not always, perhaps not even often, ultimate causes.

Speaking of proximate causes, let's say I did in fact buy that new Mercedes. When I pulled up to my home, how do you suppose I turned into my driveway? That one is easy: by turning the steering wheel. As you might expect, however, nothing is that simple when it comes to turns. My rotation of the steering wheel was only a proximate cause, which set in motion a series of cascading causes.

Turning a steering wheel rotates a shaft, which rotates a gear, which slides a rack, which moves a tie rod, which pivots the wheel, which turns on an axle, which rolls the tires, which engage with the road and turn the car. And it's even more complicated than that, as we'll explore when we examine the contest between the tire and the road in the next chapter. But this simple example highlights the principle that every turn affects other turns. Causes create effects that become other causes. Which means when we're evaluating a turn, as Daniel Findley says, "context matters."

When engineers are designing a roadway curve, they begin by examining the landscape and what it is they need to get around. If it's a single curve in the middle of nowhere, it's going to require warning signs and road markings and a slower speed limit, because it's likely to be unexpected by the driver. If it's one of a series of curves, however, it's likely something a driver can take in stride. Either way, "You can't go from perfectly straight to perfectly turned," says Findley. "At each end of a curve you would have a disruption of equilibrium."

That's a helpful way to think about the cause of any turn: it is that which disrupts equilibrium. Whether it's an overzealous baseball fan, an angry tavern owner, a driver with his hands on the steering wheel, or designers and engineers who design the cars and engineer the roads, human beings have an inordinate effect on how things in the world turn.

Take, for example, a clock. Have you ever wondered what makes it work? Hint: it's not the earth rotating on its axis. Clocks don't cause changes in time; they merely track them. All clocks are the product of human ingenuity.

The first thing a timekeeping device needs is energy, which in old-fashioned mechanical clocks is supplied by human hands turning a mainspring. As the mainspring slowly unwinds, it drives a series of interconnected gears that by turning transmit its energy to an "escapement," which acts as a turnstile that allows only one tooth of a gear to click forward, or tick, at a time. Connected to the escapement is a controller—a pendulum or a series of weights and counterweights—that controls the release of energy stored in the mainspring and keeps everything moving at a constant rate. All of that is connected to the hands on the dial that communicate to us what time it is.

It's as precise as it is ingenious, and clocks of various types differ only in the details—whether mechanical, quartz, digital, or atomic, they all rely on some form of energy to control an oscillator that provides a steady rhythm of ticking time. A clock is synchronized with the earth's rotation to provide a disruption of equilibrium at exactly one-second intervals, but its cause is the result of human intent.

It's easy to underappreciate our ability to affect the turns of our lives. It's also possible to overstate our role. The truth almost always lies in between. I recall reading the story of one Major League Baseball manager who articulated how he did everything within his power—and within the rules—to win each game. If a batter should bunt to advance the baserunners, he tells him to bunt rather than swing away. If the runner on first base can get the jump on the catcher in time to steal second, he signals in a steal. If bringing in a relief pitcher in the seventh inning helps preserve the lead, he calls the bullpen. This is not unusual, of course—these are the type of decisions every big-league manager makes. What's unusual is this particular manager's perspective. Having done all he can to win, he accepts the fact that the ball won't always bounce his way. He simply does his best to be the cause of effects he wishes to see, regardless of whether or not they come about. That perspective has enabled him to enjoy a lengthy, healthy career.

Most turns in business are like that—not entirely within our control, but not entirely beyond it, either. We may not be able to do anything about turns in the weather, but turns in a roadway, as Daniel Findley has shown us, have steadily become less perilous because of the human intent behind their design. We should approach turns in business with neither presumptive arrogance nor detached fatalism, but we mustn't be afraid to lean into them. We have a role to play.

Martin Luther didn't hesitate to lean in when his turn came, playing an outsized role in the advent of the Reformation. But his daring act on October 31, 1517, was only the Reformation's most proximate cause; as we've seen by examining the various ways to understand that moment, there were myriad other causes.

One that gets very little press is Frederick III, otherwise known as Frederick the Wise, the Duke of Saxony. Never heard of him? Well, it's likely that without him you would never have heard of Martin Luther. Historian Megan Armstrong goes so far as to say, "I don't think we would have had the Reformation in the way we had it without the Duke of Saxony."

Who was this significantly insignificant figure? A little background is in order.

When Luther nailed his ninety-five theses to the Wittenberg door, it caused quite a stir. He was summoned to the Diet of Worms, where he refused to recant, "having been granted neither his argument nor his martyrdom."[3] But he had made a lot of enemies and his life was now in danger. Once he left the protective environs of the Diet, he was on his own, and likely to be kidnapped or killed.

At that time, the Holy Roman Empire was officially ruled from Rome but practically run by a series of widely distributed, geographically based nobles, one of which was Luther sympathizer Frederick III. When Luther was returning from the Diet, Frederick staged a preemptive kidnapping and spirited Luther away to the protective walls of the Wartburg Castle. It was there that Luther translated the Bible into German and began his prodigious publishing career.

Whether Frederick's motives were born of religious devotion or the fact that Luther would continue to generate great publicity for the university he had founded in Wittenberg, we don't know. What we do know, according to Armstrong, is that "Had the Duke of Saxony not protected [Luther], history would have been very different."

Thus, Frederick the Wise could be considered just as much a cause of the Reformation as Martin Luther. As could many other people and events. There were theological questions that had been bubbling up for the previous century or more. There were long-standing ethnic tensions between Germans and Italians. There were frustrations over church taxes. There were deep cultural scars from the lingering effects of the Black Death, which was estimated to have reduced the population of Europe from seventy-three million to forty-five million in a single century. There had been a papal schism where the Catholic Church was divided between two and three popes. And not insignificantly, there was the Renaissance.

Dating the moment of the Renaissance is as challenging as dating the moment of the Reformation, but generally speaking, it took place between the fourteenth and seventeenth centuries.

It was a period of rediscovery of the cultural, political, and artistic achievements of the Greek and Roman periods, of da Vinci and Erasmus and Copernicus and Galileo, of Dante, Michelangelo, Shakespeare, and Chaucer.

Of the Renaissance, Armstrong says, "The turn was to go back to what was better, a more authentic past. The idea was that the Renaissance was restorative; it was going back to this epoch. Going to the past becomes a source of reinvention."[4] This pattern, turning to the past to reform the future, was also the path of the Reformation.

"The Renaissance gave western Christendom a slogan: *ad fontes*, 'to the sources,' an urge to return to the ancient, and therefore pure, founts of truth," says Alec Ryrie. "By 1500, this fashion for antiquity was sweeping into every field of knowledge."[5] This was the environment in which Luther had grown up, and it clearly had an impact on him and his desire "not to try to modernize the world but to save it."[6] It was the cultural milieu in which his desire to go back to the Bible, the apostolic age, and the early church fathers like Augustine had been nurtured.

As the turn of the Reformation was caused in part by the turn of the Renaissance, it in turn and in part led to the Enlightenment in the seventeenth and eighteenth centuries. Two individuals in particular, Francis Bacon and Isaac Newton, were most influential during this time; Joel Mokyr creatively describes them as "cultural entrepreneurs."[7]

Entrepreneur is a term familiar to all of us in a twenty-first-century capitalist economy. Borrowed from the French, *entrepreneur* originally meant "one who undertakes or manages." In modern usage it has come to refer to a person who undertakes and manages a business, bearing the risk and reaping the rewards.

I have cofounded two companies, but I never wanted to be an entrepreneur, having little stomach for risk. The turn to becoming my own boss was caused by an unanticipated sequence of events. I was happily employed at a company where I had risen to the position of president, and in due time I was offered an opportunity to buy out the founder. Taking ownership in a going concern where I was already firmly rooted felt about right to me—I could enjoy all the benefits of being an owner without having to risk my life savings (meager as they were) on a startup. But after four years of trying, the deal fell through, and I found myself having to leave the firm.

At that point I had two choices: go to work for another company or launch my own. After much reflection I realized I had enjoyed so much freedom and responsibility in my previous position that I just didn't think I could work for someone else. Starting my own company, it turned out, actually appeared to be the lower-risk option—particularly if I could do it with a trusted partner. It was the single most consequential turn in my professional life, and its cause was beyond my control. I've enjoyed the rewards of entrepreneurship, but to do so I also had to bear the risks.

As did Bacon and Newton. Mokyr defines cultural entrepreneurs as "people who become influential to the point where they change the culture of a sufficiently large number of others to affect their behavior and eventually institutions in significant ways."[8] He puts Luther in the same category, aided by the fact that in the post-1500 European environment it was more difficult for various regimes to suppress heretics. Not only was there increasing disagreement on exactly what a heretic was, but the rise of nationalism splintered traditional power centers and created unique political and religious rivalries across whose borders controversial characters could flow.

The status quo was increasingly giving way to innovation in all three men's cases. Their respected reputations today are the just rewards of their efforts, but only because they were willing to bear the risks of thinking differently in their time.

Francis Bacon was, according to Thomas Jefferson, one of the three greatest men who ever lived. He was born only fifteen years after Martin Luther's death, but into a whole new world. Bacon rose through a series of political appointments to earn the lofty title of Lord Chancellor of England and knighthood. At the age of sixty he retired after an inauspicious collapse of his political career and devoted himself to his avocation, the philosophy of science. He became the father of the scientific method as a natural outgrowth of his faith, believing that "Knowledge is the rich storehouse for the glory of the Creator and the relief of man's estate."[9]

Bacon's synthesis of religion and science represented a turn in human events that had never before been seen. In Bacon's mind, an empirical and experimental approach to discovering the truths about the world was a way of pursuing "good works," not only as an aid in helping understand God but in helping his fellow man. "The true and lawful goal of the sciences is simply this," said Bacon, "that human life be enriched by new discoveries and powers."[10] This led to the flourishing of science as never before.

Baconianism was then, in Mokyr's words, "subsumed in Newtonianism" and a "growing conviction that science should serve the purpose of economic progress." In an echo of Bacon's birth just years after Luther, Newton was born a mere fifteen years after Bacon's death.

Like Bacon, Newton believed the physical world was intelligible, understandable, and governed by natural law, all set in motion by the First Cause. As he wrote regarding the planets in the epilogue to his seventeenth-century three-volume masterpiece, *Philosophiæ Naturalis Principia Mathematica* (Mathematical Principles of Natural Philosophy), "Though these bodies may indeed persevere in their orbits by the mere laws of gravity, yet they could by no means have at first deriv'd the regular position of the orbits themselves from those laws."[11]

If it was God who set the laws of nature in motion, Newton believed, it would be to the glory of God that they be discovered. He took the flicker of the scientific method and over a lifetime of study and invention fanned it into a flame of the Scientific Revolution, most notably in the fields of physics and mathematics—if you hated high school calculus, you have Newton to blame. Newton's First Law of Motion lies at the core of this exploration of the causes of turns. It states that an object at rest will remain at rest unless acted upon by an external force.

That's as applicable to human affairs as it is to the motion of the planets or an apple falling from a tree. Sometimes we may be the "object at rest" and other times the "external force," but we should never be surprised when our equilibrium gets disrupted. It's just how the universe works. But we can almost always play a role in how events unfold, with Newton himself serving as an excellent example. His impact on the turns of science and human progress is impossible to calculate, but Mokyr provides a fitting summary:

> Perhaps the most important contribution that Newton's work made to the Industrial Enlightenment was the elegance and completeness with which he explained

> phenomena and regularities that had puzzled people for centuries. The point was not just that his equations, which explained celestial motions as well as provided a theoretical basis for much that had been known before on the motions of earthly bodies and the behavior of light, provided a world of order and logic. It was also the Baconian ideal of understanding nature through observation and experiment and thus its control seemed so much closer. In the age of Enlightenment, Newton became the epitome of the potential of human rationality. Newton's work filled other scholars with hope that areas such as farming, medicine, chemistry, electricity, materials, and even the "science of man" would soon be similarly reduced to well-understood elegant laws.[12]

It would be oversimplifying to suggest that Luther's cause led to Bacon's effect, Bacon's cause led to Newton's effect, and Newton's cause led to so many effects they can't be counted. But can we be certain Newton would have become Newton without Bacon's example? Or that Bacon would have become Bacon without Luther's influence? Those are unanswerable questions, of course, but as Clarence the angel said to a despondent George Bailey in *It's a Wonderful Life*, "Strange, isn't it? Each man's life touches so many other lives."[13] One turn always leads to another, and the causes of turns, both proximate and tangential, are often interrelated.

Causes beyond my control have led to both triumph and trouble for my company, but I have learned that what appears to be a good turn doesn't always play out that way, nor does a bad one always result in a negative outcome. What I do in response to initial causes almost always makes a difference. As the

Greek Stoic philosopher Epictetus said, "It's not what happens to you, but how you react to it that matters." Where we're born, and when, and under what circumstances may set the table for our lives, but we have much to say about the meal.

Adam Smith's life overlapped with Isaac Newton's by a mere four years, but his thinking was greatly affected by the giant of science. Smith studied Newton as a student at Glasgow University, characterizing in one essay Newton's insights regarding how the solar system works as "the greatest discovery that ever was made by man."[14] Believing that Newtonian thinking could apply across all areas of scientific discovery, Smith set out to apply the idea of a discoverable order to social and economic systems. As the Scientific Revolution was turning into the Industrial Revolution, Smith took on the task of explaining what was happening, and why, from the perspective of economics.

This turn had been long in coming. Centuries of feudalism had slowly given way to a rebirth of markets like those that had flourished in ancient Greece and Rome, enhanced by increasing scientific discoveries such as crop rotation and windmills and labor-saving devices such as improved plows and the raising of livestock, which required fewer laborers than growing crops on the same acreage. This, along with religious change and shifting political power, enabled some members of the lower classes to take permanent leave of the manors to which they had long been tied and become traveling merchants.

Mercantile economies in Spain, Portugal, France, and England began importing more gold and silver, the coinage of which made trade easier. Advances in weaponry like the English longbow, gunpowder, and canons further enabled the rise of nation-states and the corresponding demise of the need for mastery of the sword, the traditional realm of knights and manors. Markets for products, services, and labor began to flourish, as did the sale of indulgences, Martin Luther's original complaint. Merchants, up-enders of the status quo upon whom nobles and high churchmen looked with disdain, felt an alliance with the antiestablishment thrust of Protestantism and its favorable view of hard work, frugality, and trade-based prosperity. The "Protestant work ethic" was emerging.

"Over some six centuries," says economic historian E. Ray Canterbery, "the forces that would guarantee the establishment of and justification for competitive market economics in much of Western Europe were grinding away at the economic roots of the manor and the political organization of feudalism."[15]

By Smith's time, Great Britain had become the world's wealthiest and most powerful nation, creating for the first time a "middle class" whose occupations were increasingly a form of economic specialization and for whom trade for food, clothing, entertainment, and other necessities of life was increasingly normalized. While the nation's rulers had continued their preoccupation with conquest and the acquisition of precious metals, Smith recognized that true wealth was not measured in money but in that which money can buy—goods and services. It was these, not storehouses of gold and silver, that comprised "the wealth of nations."

Canterbery characterizes the causes of this turn using a wide historical lens. "Expanding commerce had brought a measure of liberty and security to individuals," he says. "People whose forebears had lived in servile dependency upon royal masters and suffered continual warfare saw feudalism breaking down with the rise of a money exchange economy. Smith spoke of the beneficence of the Newtonian universe, of new liberties through natural law, and of the necessity for release from the arbitrariness of government, all of which found an eager, receptive audience in England, France, and elsewhere."[16]

This marked the beginning of the Industrial Revolution, as evidenced by an increasing velocity of new advances in science such as the discovery of iron and steel alloys and the invention of the steam engine, which exponentially reduced the need for human labor and led to productivity-enhancing developments as varied as steamships, locomotives, and ever-larger factories.

We tend not to think about these (relatively recent) historical turns as we go about designing and manufacturing, pricing and promoting, and selling and servicing our own companies' wares, and we take for granted the relatively light touch the governing authorities place on our businesses. Though there will always be debate regarding business taxes and regulatory policy, we've come a long way from our mercantilist and feudalist past. In those days, the causes of most economic turns were in the hands of kings and nobles; today they're largely in our own.

Adam Smith's most famous work, *An Inquiry into the Nature and Causes of the Wealth of Nations*, explained how individuals and corporate entities, acting solely in their own interests and constrained by competition, would, by an "invisible hand," improve economic conditions for all. In Smithian philosophy, private property is as necessary to a working economy as it is moral, capital can be productive as investment, the division of labor increases prosperity for all, incentives matter, trade is good, and profits are a measure of how well one is meeting others' needs. He didn't call it capitalism—that term would be first popularized as a slur by Karl Marx almost a hundred years later—but he was the first to recognize it.

Scientifically and economically speaking, the world has been turning faster ever since, as one discovery has led to another in an endless stream of learning and invention, protected (to one extent or another and in varying degrees in varying places) by morality and the rule of law. Innovations as simple as the 1884 invention of the light switch, which completes an electric circuit with a simple turn of a lever, enabled tremendous advancements in safety, productivity, and quality of life.

Along the way a lot of companies have come and gone, and a great many fortunes have been won and lost, but the increasing understanding of how market economies work and mounting evidence of their ability to improve human flourishing has fueled a spirit of entrepreneurialism that doesn't merely wonder how progress happens or wait for it to unfold, but actively works to bring it about. The realization that change is not only a fact of life but can be actively initiated may have been slow in coming, but once it dawned on opportunistic inventors it unleashed a flurry of innovation.

A contemporary of Adam Smith, Jean-Baptiste Say, captured this thinking with his "Law of Markets," which in shorthand can be characterized as "supply creates its own demand." Say observed that in order to have the means to purchase goods or services, buyers must first have produced something to sell. Therefore, production is the key to economic growth and, absent government interference, production will lead to the increasing prosperity of individuals and wealth of nations.

Say's Law has been in evidence ever since, as new products and services which nobody asked for, and in many cases never even dreamed of, have enhanced the lives of millions. *Time* magazine once cataloged what it called "The 50 Most Influential Gadgets of All Time," among them the transistor radio, the Polaroid Camera, the Commodore 64 computer, the answering machine, GPS, and the VCR.[17] How the editors were able to reduce literally millions of inventions to the fifty most influential I don't know, but they missed one that can be found in almost every kitchen in America (and most dorm rooms): the microwave oven.

The phrase "Nobody ever asked for a microwave oven" could be said of many innovations, but in the case of the microwave it was literally true. Shortly after the end of WWII, a Raytheon engineer named Percy Spencer observed that his nearby peanut cluster bar had melted while he was testing a magnetron, a device that creates electromagnetic waves. Curious about what had happened, Spencer ran another test using an egg, which promptly exploded, followed by popcorn, a freshly popped batch of which he shared with his colleagues. A year later, the Radarange, the first commercially available microwave oven, was introduced to the public.[18] Spencer's accident had been the cause whose effect would save millions of families billions of hours in the kitchen—time that could be devoted to other pursuits.

Among those pursuits was an explosion in leisure-time activities, resulting in increasing twists and turns (sometimes of knees and ankles) among an increasingly active, increasingly aging population. Enter Masaki Watanabe, a Japanese orthopedist and inventor who developed a slim, telescoping lens with which he could peer into his patients' damaged joints.

"Arthroscopy," as it has come to be known, was soon expanded beyond diagnosis to treatment, enabling much simpler, less dangerous surgeries and significantly shorter recovery times. Most arthroscopic operations today are performed as outpatient surgery and have led to dramatic enhancements and extensions of the careers of both professional and amateur athletes. As was true of the microwave, nobody ever asked to have their knee, shoulder, elbow, or wrist "scoped" before such a procedure existed.

Microwave popcorn and outpatient surgery notwithstanding, economic progress since the time of Smith and Say has not been uninterrupted. There have been more than forty economic downturns since then, from the "Panic of 1785" in the wake of the American Revolution to the "Panic of 1857" just prior to the Civil War, and from the "Great Depression" of the 1930s to the "Great Recession" that dominated the early years of the twenty-first century. Not to mention the unprecedented shutting down of the global economy in response to a novel coronavirus that made its debut in 2019 and the raging inflation that followed.

Recessions and depressions are natural "turns" of the economic cycle and are the result of a variety of causes, including fluctuations in interest rates, consumer demand, production, and employment. These can in turn be triggered by external events such as war, weather, and pandemics and exacerbated by human intervention, from centralized government policies to decentralized rumors and panic.

Looking back on each downturn, it's possible to point to one or more proximate causes, such as the stock market crash of 1929 or the bursting of the housing bubble in 2007. However, economic turns, like historical turns, are the result of a variety of intertwined events. You might say the business cycle is entirely predictable, other than its timing, which makes it entirely unpredictable.

This is no less true of turns in individual industries. Nobody can predict when a new technology will upset the status quo; Nokia had 42 percent market share in cellular phones when Apple released the iPhone, and *Fortune* magazine declared

Yahoo! the victor in the "search wars" before Google was even incorporated. But every business leader knows that, to survive long term, as Harvard's Levitt put it, "they themselves will have to plot the obsolescence of what now produces their livelihood."

That's a fair way of describing the implications of what economic historian Joseph Schumpeter first called "creative destruction." The invention of the automobile put the horse-and-buggy manufacturers out of business. The invention of the telegraph put the Pony Express out of business. And the invention of the internet put more mom-and-pop companies than can be counted out of business.

It also led to more mom-and-pop startups than ever, which is the "creative" part of creative destruction and a good reminder that we can be active participants in each unfolding turn. One way to overcome creative destruction is through creative disruption, choosing to be an agent of change rather than a victim of it. To be the cause rather than the effect.

Pause for a moment on that thought. Creative destruction is a fact of life in business. Whatever your industry and no matter your success, how you operate today will be disrupted. It may be sooner or it may be later, it may be by increments or it may be all at once, but it will change. You have the choice to either drive that change or be driven by it. Some people might find that intimidating; I consider it invigorating and empowering.

It's the choice Doug Pruitt was confronted with when Sundt Corporation, like so many companies before and since, was contending with the forces of creative destruction. The company was perilously close to becoming a statistic. "What drove the turn was fear," said Pruitt, describing his thought process at the time. "If we don't start doing stuff dramatically, not tinkering around the edges, but doing stuff dramatically, we're going to be gone."

At a management retreat, Pruitt pulled back the covers and revealed to his entire team where the company was financially. He told those gathered, "If you don't understand today, you'll never understand where we are. We're broke. We're going to make an incredible amount of changes here, and many of you are not going to like them." Crisis was the cause of Sundt's turn.

Pruitt went on to explain that the company had been stuck in an old paradigm, believing that owning even underutilized assets was better than leasing them. But those underutilized assets meant that crucial capital was tied up in areas where it couldn't be productive. "We continued to dig, looking for things to fix, close, or sell that would bring in money and move us away from the edge of the abyss," he says. "Sundt seemed to be drowning in divisions that hadn't been profitable in years. We had land that was just sitting there, and cash-draining assets that we continued to own."[19]

The bad news is all of this put Sundt in near-death condition. The good news is it could be changed by the company returning to the entrepreneurial spirit and careful expense management of its past.

That's a prescription my firm gives to many companies when they find themselves dealing with a downturn—to return to first principles, to rediscover and recommit to why they were founded so they can clarify what to cling to and what to let go of. The ability to hold firmly to their mission yet loosely to their model gives company leaders the freedom they need to make often significant adjustments as they navigate industry and economic turns. The "cause" upon which they were founded can be the strong foundation on which to base a necessary and productive turn.

Throughout history a lot of forward progress has come as the result of hearkening back. It's no accident that the prefix of both Renaissance and Reformation is *re*, a Latin root that means "again." There's a Greek term, *metanoia*, that over the centuries has been translated in a handful of different ways, from "transformation" to "penance." As the Reformation was dawning in 1535, William Tyndale translated the Bible to English—for which he was rewarded with a death sentence—and chose to render *metanoia* as the English word "repent." To *repent*, in the simplest terms, simply means "to turn." *Repent*, *renew*, and *reassess* all suggest a way to move forward by looking to the past. As do more corporate terms such as *retain*, *refocus*, *retool*, *retrain*, *redeploy*, and *renegotiate*.

Resolute is one of those words that, unfortunately, could be used to characterize both sides of the Civil War conflagration. Despite all the political and economic advances of the previous centuries, despite the increasing wealth and industrial power their neighbors to the North were enjoying, plantation owners in the American South stubbornly held on to their inhumane practice of slavery. And abolitionists in the North were just as resolute in their determination to end it.

One proximate cause of the war was the Missouri Compromise of 1820, which admitted Missouri as a slave state and Maine as a free state and only heightened the tensions between North and South. The expansion of slavery it permitted, an aging Thomas Jefferson said, was "like a fireball in the night" that "awakened and filled me with terror."[20] He knew a tragic confrontation lay ahead.

Perhaps the most proximate cause of the start of the war was the election of Abraham Lincoln as president. The campaign of 1860 wasn't a typical presidential contest; Lincoln ran on a platform specifically opposed to the expansion of slavery, and the Southern states knew it. In his first inaugural address, the newly elected president put the matter plainly: "One section of our country believes slavery is right and ought to be extended, while the other believes it is wrong, and ought not to be extended. This is the only substantial dispute."[21] Thirty-nine days later, the Confederates fired on Fort Sumter.

As with all turns, the causes of the Civil War and its ultimate outcome were many and interrelated. Changes in public opinion were among the more notable, and consequential, ones.

Initially, Americans in the North were bullish on the war and expected a quick and complete victory. They were stunned by the early tactical successes and subsequent perseverance of the Southern forces, and as the war dragged on and bodies piled up, confidence in the Union effort began to flag. This was a significant factor that led to Lincoln's September 22, 1862, issuance of the Emancipation Proclamation declaring all slaves in the Confederate states "then, thenceforward, and forever free" as of the following January 1.

Despite his opposition to slavery, Lincoln hadn't believed to that point that the federal government had the authority under the Constitution to completely abolish it, only to prevent its expansion. He had written earlier in 1862 that his "paramount objective" was to save the Union, not to destroy slavery everywhere it existed. But he also wrote, "If I could save [the Union] by freeing all the slaves I would do it."[22] He may have been tipping his hand that his calculus had evolved over the preceding bloody year, sensing that the proclamation would be a way to galvanize public opinion and inject new life into the Union cause.

On New Year's Day 1863, Lincoln signed the Emancipation Proclamation, calling it "my greatest and most enduring contribution to the history of the war, the central act of my administration, and the great event of the 19th Century." He added, "I never in my life felt more certain that I was doing right than I do in signing this paper. If my name ever goes into history, it will be for this act, and my whole soul is in it."[23]

With the Union victory it would help inspire, the Emancipation Proclamation enabled Lincoln to accomplish both of his goals, the preservation of the Union and the abolition of slavery, reflected in the moving final words of the Gettysburg Address given months later that "this nation, under God, shall have a new birth of freedom—and that government of the people, by the people, for the people, shall not perish from the earth."

Public opinion has been crucial in many other historical turns. It was galvanized by the Boston Tea Party, a largely symbolic event that united the American colonists against the abuses of the British Crown. It was the prize sought by Mark Hanna in his masterful shaping of William McKinley's image in the election of 1896. Public opinion was fused by Japan's December 7, 1941, attack on Pearl Harbor, turning an unpopular war across the seas into an American cause. And it was stunned by the 1945 dropping of atomic bombs on Hiroshima and Nagasaki, events that turned Japan's commitment to fighting to the last man into unconditional surrender.

"Alarm" may have been the best way to characterize public opinion in 1957 when the Soviet Union launched Sputnik, reinforcing fears that Eastern Bloc Communists were winning the Cold War and leading President Kennedy to commit to landing a man on the moon by the end of the 1960s. And public opinion was decisive in Lyndon Johnson's victory over Barry Goldwater in 1964 with an almost unprecedented 61 percent of the popular vote—in part due to a bipartisan advance in the lingering and unfinished turn from slavery that post–Civil War Reconstruction had failed to fully address. Causes do not have to be proximate to be powerful.

Johnson had a leg up in the campaign from the start, having ascended to the office after the tragic assassination of President Kennedy in late 1963. Sympathies for Johnson were still running high a year after his sudden appointment, as Americans sought a return to normalcy. And the president was also riding the wave of having his signature legislation, the Civil Rights Act of 1964, pass Congress (with greater support from the opposition party than from his own) almost a hundred years after the end of the Civil War.

But Goldwater was undeterred, based on his preoccupation with the global balance of power. A staunch anti-Communist during the height of the Cold War, Goldwater represented the hawkish wing of the hawkish wing. "I would remind you that extremism in the defense of liberty is no vice," he famously said during the campaign, and "moderation in the pursuit of justice is no virtue." He was against the Nuclear Test Ban Treaty and was not entirely unopposed to the use of nuclear weapons in Vietnam, should it come to that.

Johnson had an inside track to victory, but it was not guaranteed until he aired a single television commercial, a single time, on September 7, 1964, which crystallized public opinion and sealed Goldwater's fate. The ad, titled "Daisy," featured a little girl picking petals off a flower and counting them as she did. "One, two," she said, as the camera slowly zoomed in on her cherubic face. "Three, four," she continued.

When she got to ten, her sweet voice was drowned out by the ominous overtones of an official countdown: "Ten, nine, eight, seven, six," the countdown began, the camera continuing to zoom in closer on the girl. "Five, four, three, two, one," the announcer said, as viewers now saw in the iris of her eye a startling atomic explosion.

As the mushroom cloud ballooned toward the sky, President Johnson's voice-over delivered the final blow: "These are the stakes," he said. "To make a world in which all of God's children can live, or to go into the dark." He wrapped it up by paraphrasing a 1939 W. H. Auden line, which the poet himself had since disavowed: "We must either love each other, or we must die."[24] An authoritative voice then intoned, "Vote for President Johnson on November 3rd. The stakes are too high for you to stay home."[25]

By today's standards the ad was relatively tame. But in 1964, nothing like it had ever been seen on television. The national newscasts replayed the ad as a news story, and those sixty seconds convinced many remaining swing voters that Goldwater could not be trusted to have his finger on the nuclear trigger. It not only turned the opinions of the electorate, but as is the case with other turns that have consequences beyond their original intent, it also represented a turn toward the accusatory and deceptive political advertising we're still dealing with today.

Yet Johnson's turn in the barrel was coming. Just four years later, after the successful passage of his Great Society legislation creating Medicare and Medicaid (both of which represented complex turns with complicated consequences of their own), he made a stunning announcement on national television: "I shall not seek, and I will not accept, the nomination of my party for another term as your President."[26]

The war in Vietnam had taken its toll on the country, and the "nation's newsman," Walter Cronkite, publicly criticized the war effort. On his February 27, 1968, broadcast, Cronkite shared his dour view that, "It seems now more certain than ever that the bloody experience of Vietnam is to end in a stalemate." Regarding that broadcast, which aired just weeks before his announcement that he wouldn't seek another term, Johnson said, "If I've lost Cronkite, I've lost Middle America."[27]

Johnson's eventful five years as president demonstrate that causes of turns are complex and often misunderstood. MIT meteorology professor Edward Lorenz made this point through a thought-provoking question he posed at a scientific conference in the 1960s: "Does the flap of a butterfly's wings in Brazil set off a tornado in Texas?" His contention was not that the most innocuous of actions can set in motion an unstoppable chain of events (as the "Butterfly Effect" has come to be understood in popular culture), but that the world is too complex to posit simple cause-and-effect relationships. Each cause affects all the others, and there's no way of ultimately cataloging all the varying interrelationships.

That said, unlike butterflies in Brazil, human beings can think consequentially. Our minds are exquisitely tuned to pick up detail. We have intelligence and foresight. We can pursue knowledge and gain insight. We can see patterns in events both big and small, current and historical, and we can connect dots.

That's what Kerry Livgren's wife did, and the result is one of the bestselling records of all time. Livgren, the founder and musical genius behind the rock group Kansas, was working on a follow-up album to *Leftoverture*, the band's first big taste of commercial success and five-time platinum record. A self-described "rock-and-roll electric guitar player," Livgren wasn't comfortable with his skills on the acoustic guitar. At home one day he was trying to improve his proficiency by making up a musical exercise to teach himself to fingerpick.

He says, "I was sitting in my music room, playing this thing, and my wife walked by. She stood there and listened for a second, and she goes, 'Boy, that's really pretty—you should [put] words with that.'" Livgren explained that he was just doing an exercise, to which she responded, "No, no—that's really nice—don't forget that now."

When Livgren and the band were finishing up rehearsals prior to recording their next album, they were looking for one more song. Livgren hesitantly told them, "Well, I've got this one, but you guys wouldn't like it. I mean, this is not Kansas." He played it for his bandmates and they loved it. Over Livgren's continued protests ("I didn't think it was a Kansas-type song"), "Dust in the Wind" was born. It went on to become the band's best-known song, appearing on the country and easy listening as well as rock charts and exposing Kansas to a much broader audience.[28]

Was the "cause" of "Dust in the Wind" Livgren's desire to master the acoustic guitar? Was it his sheer musical talent? Was it his wife's attentive ear or relentless urging? His band's need for one more song? His inability to convince them that it didn't fit their style? All of the above, and more. Prior to the music unfolding, Livgren stumbled across the lyric as he struggled with his life's meaning:

> I was reading a book on American Indian poetry one day, and I came across that line . . . "For all we are is dust in the wind." And I thought, well, you know, that's

> really true. Here I've got all this success—I've got material possessions, I've got a goal in my life that had been accomplished at that point, but I'm going back into the ground, and what does this really mean in light of that? And that's really kind of the message of that song.

Apparently, he wasn't the only person who needed to hear it, and the world of music was enriched because of the way he turned his fingers one day on the neck of his guitar.

The Law of Causality is a philosophical concept dating all the way back to Aristotle. It says that every effect must have an antecedent cause. That's not to say that effects can't have multiple causes, nor that causes can't result in multiple effects. But an effect is, by definition, something that has a cause, and a cause is something that results in an effect.

Take some time and do some "turn forensics" on your company and industry. Just as you reflected on various ways to conceive of the moment in which your organization finds itself, consider the causes of the turns of events that led it to where it is. Which of those did you initiate, and which were beyond your control? Which were intentional and which fortuitous? Which played out as expected and which were a surprise? Why?

And consider the turns your company, your competitors, or some kid tinkering in a garage may be initiating today. What, or who, is causing them? What are the historical or existing turns by which they're prefaced? What are not only their likely first-order consequences, but second- and third- as well? How must things unfold for them to be successful? What is your company's role in the mix? One way of conceiving of strategy is that it is simply the initiation of and response to turns—in culture, in consumer preferences, in technology, in the economy.

If you see a turn coming, get out in front of it. If you see a turn is needed, make it happen.

Without a sculptor, there can be no statue. Without an author, there can be no book. Without an inventor, there can be no invention. Without an entrepreneur, there can be no company. Without what happened yesterday, today wouldn't be what it is. And how tomorrow unfolds is entirely dependent on what happens today.

Like dust in the wind, the causes of turns may arise from places we can't see and create effects we don't anticipate. But that doesn't make us irrelevant. If we listen, and watch, and remain alert, we'll be better prepared to recognize turns as they begin to reveal themselves. We'll be more adept at understanding why they may be happening. And we'll be better able to direct their course, becoming a cause of the effects we wish to see.

> ***The Principle of the Cause***
> *People aren't the cause of every turn, but we can be a cause in every turn (and often an instrumental one).*

CONTESTS

"I can't keep up with your turning tables."
Adele

War. Religion. Politics. Sports. Business. In every arena, a turn is a contest of competing forces.

Whether it's Unionists vs. Confederates, Protestants vs. Catholics, Bryan vs. McKinley, Cubs vs. Marlins, or a company vs. its competitors, turns of events share the same dynamics as turns in our physical world: force acts against force until, through victory or standoff, some new state of equilibrium arises.

Richard Rumelt of the UCLA Anderson School of Management is a world-renowned management expert whom the *McKinsey Quarterly* once called "strategy's strategist." He says, "The most important element of a strategy is a coherent viewpoint about the forces at work, not a plan."[1] It's easy to get ahead of ourselves when we're confronted with change, becoming preoccupied with trying to determine the best plan of attack. But if our viewpoint about the forces at work isn't coherent—or is off by even a few degrees—our plans are likely to end in disappointment. Or worse.

Developing a coherent viewpoint about the forces at work in the physical world was one of the great contributions of Isaac

Newton, which is why forces in nature are measured in units called "newtons" even today. Newton's Three Laws of Motion forever changed the way we look at our world. His First Law of Motion (inertia) is the principle that an object in motion will remain in motion unless acted upon by another force. When it is acted upon by another force, however, something's got to give. In many cases, what gives is the direction in which the object is heading. The result is a turn.

The earth is an object in motion, hurtling through space at a velocity of almost 67,000 miles per hour. According to Newton's First Law, we should be heading off in a single direction forever, away from the light and warmth of the sun. Fortunately, the law of gravity says that objects attract one another in proportion to their mass, so the sun keeps us from straying too far away. And it just so happens that the earth is traveling at the exact speed necessary to counteract the sun's gravitational pull. Any slower and we'd turn into that solar goo mentioned in Chapter One, and any faster and we'd shoot off into dark, cold deep space.[2] This is one contest where a standoff is exactly what we need.

The same drama plays out beyond our solar system at the galactic level. We've already seen that all the galaxies beyond the Milky Way are continually spinning. Were they not, their own internal gravity would cause them to collapse into black holes. Then all those black holes would collapse into one another, forming one giant black hole into which everything else would collapse—including our perfectly tuned solar system.[3]

This "fine tuning" of the universe makes it appear as if it had been specifically designed for life, which Bacon and Newton took for granted. What they didn't know at the time, given that they were plying their trades at the front end of the Scientific

Revolution, were the details. We have since learned, for example, that if the earth were farther from or closer to the sun, there would be no water cycle. Should the time it takes the earth to rotate on its axis be longer, the days would be too hot and the nights too cold to support life. If gravity were any stronger on earth, our atmosphere would contain too much methane and ammonia; if it were weaker, we wouldn't have enough rainfall. Were the crust of the earth to be thicker, there would be too little oxygen in the atmosphere; were it to be thinner, the tectonic plates would be unstable and volcanic activity unbearable.

Not to mention the moon, which is not only critical to the tides but to many other aspects of life on earth. Astronomer Donald Brownlee and paleontologist Peter Ward expressed this thought rather poetically when they wrote, "Without the Moon there would be no moonbeams, no month, no lunacy, no Apollo program, less poetry, and a world where every night was dark and gloomy. Without the Moon it is also likely that no birds, redwoods, whales, trilobite, or other advanced life would ever grace the earth."[4] Various and competing forces are involved in every turn we make, scientific and poetic, conspiring to keep us in equilibrium. Which in astronomical terms, at least, is a good thing.

Two big forces we often hear about are centripetal force and centrifugal force. If you're like me, you can never keep them straight in your mind. Centripetal (Latin for "center seeking") force is the force that pulls an object in toward the center of a turn, like the sun tugging on the earth. Centrifugal (Latin for "center fleeing") force is the opposite—the force that fights the turn.

The source of the centripetal force depends on the object in question. For planets in orbit, the force comes from gravity. When a tetherball is being swung around a pole, the force is provided by tension in the rope. In the case of a spinning top, the force is provided by internal stress. A car moving through a curve generates centripetal force as a result of friction between the tires and the road. So far, so good.

But here's where it gets confusing: centrifugal force, which is theoretically the opposite of centripetal force, isn't really a force at all. Whether it causes mud to fly off the tires or the feeling of being thrown against your car door when rounding a sharp curve, centrifugal force is merely the inertia that wants you to keep going in a straight line. It's centripetal force looking in the mirror and believing its reflection is real.

Consider the automotive example. Say a car is traveling in a straight line at forty miles per hour. That means the driver is also traveling in a straight line at forty miles per hour. When he initiates a right turn, the causes that cascade from his turn of the steering wheel create friction between the car's tires and the road, resulting in a turn. But according to Newton's First Law of Motion, though the car is turning, the driver will continue to move in a straight line until acted upon by an external force—in this case, the car door. Rather than centrifugal force throwing him into the door, centripetal force is throwing the door into him. It's just not getting the credit for it.

This is important because it demonstrates how deceptive the forces in a turn can be. Our senses can fool us. The sun doesn't really rise in the morning and set at night; it's the earth's rotation that causes the illusion of the sun rising and setting, in the same way that centripetal force causes the illusion of driver being thrown into door, rather than door into driver. If a company's revenue is in decline, is it because it's doing something wrong, or its competitor is doing something right? If turnover is up, is it due to an unhealthy culture or a healthy job market? It's not always easy to tell, and if we react to the onset of a turn based on feelings and fears, we can easily make a mistake. Understanding the various forces at work enables us to adjust accordingly when we're caught off balance.

Newton's Second Law states that force equals mass times acceleration. The bigger an object is, and the faster it's accelerating, the more force it will exert. This is why a 245-pound linebacker in full blitz will emerge victorious from a collision with a 180-pound running back who's just getting the handoff.

Newton's Third Law, that for every action there's an equal and opposite reaction, is why that running back will end up no longer running and on his back. The forces generated by the collision turn his forward motion backwards—and if he fumbles, will have caused a turnover as well.

No matter the arena (or stadium, as it were), the forces involved in turns can be instructive.

Momentum is one that has already come up in the football analogy. The more momentum an object has, the more difficult it is to stop; had the running back had a chance to accelerate and catch the linebacker on his heels, their roles may have been reversed. Similarly, momentum can be an aid in turning; just as it's easier for a car moving at highway speed to change lanes than for one at a near standstill, a tailback running at full speed can turn on a dime.

The running back's turn is enabled by friction (otherwise known as traction) between his cleats and the grass, similar to the friction between a car's tires and the road. When two objects come into contact, friction is the resistance to motion they have relative to one another. Technically, friction is the result of electromagnetic attraction between the two surfaces; like lint and your best dark slacks, they kind of like sticking together. Practically, friction makes pretty much everything we do possible.

Without friction, not only would cars not be able to turn, they wouldn't stay on the road at all because their tires would slip and slide until the car ended up in the ditch. Riding a bike? Same problem—forget it. Walking wouldn't even work, because our shoes wouldn't be able to sustain any grip on the ground. For that matter, without friction it would be impossible to crawl, stand up, keep our pants on, or even eat, because neither fingers nor fork would be able to pick up food. It goes back to the First Law of Motion; without the countervailing force of friction, anything that was able to get moving would keep moving forever. Thus, friction in nature is often very good. In human relations? We'll get to that.

There are two types of friction, one that limits how fast things move against one another (kinetic friction), and one that keeps things right where they are (static friction). Kinetic friction is why all but the heaviest suitcases coming off the airport conveyor belt tend to gently slide down the baggage carousel. Static friction is why the lightest suitcases sit at the top until they get bumped lower. Interestingly, the smallest force required to start something in motion is always greater than the force required to continue its motion.

That's a helpful truism to remember when you're faced with a heavy lift. Columnist Andree Seu tells the story of a woman she ran into bagging groceries who is the mother of five in addition to raising several foster children. When Seu asked the woman how she managed to do it all, her answer was simple and direct: "I do the next thing that needs to be done."[5] Friction is strongest when something isn't moving; lean into it and it's not so bad. And when you do get things moving, don't be surprised that kinetic friction causes some of its energy to be converted into heat. More on that soon, too.

Leverage is another force associated with a turn. Recall how the big brains at MIT provided a helpful example of a moment occurring when someone pushes on a door causing it to turn? Well, if you push on that door near the hinges, it requires more force to open than if you push on it at the doorknob three feet farther from the hinges. The width of the door provides more leverage. This comes at the cost of having to cover more ground; at the hinges a door must only move a few inches to go from closed to open, whereas at the handle it must travel several feet. But leverage makes that distance a lot easier to cover.

We use leverage all the time to make turns less difficult. A crowbar makes it easier to open a stuck door or yank a nail, and the longer the bar, the more the leverage it provides. A wheelbarrow employs leverage to help its user lift and turn large loads. The handle of a hammer provides leverage, too—it's a whole lot easier to pound a nail holding the handle than holding the head. Same with an axe vs. an axe head and debt vs. equity financing. The Greek mathematician and inventor Archimedes said given a place to stand with a long enough lever, he could move the world.

And then there's torque, which is a special kind of leverage associated with turns. Torque is a Latin word meaning "twist," and the simplest way to define it is the ability of something to overcome rotational turning resistance. Think of how much easier it is to turn a screw with a screwdriver than with your fingers, or to turn your car using the steering wheel. And just as a longer lever can increase the force on an object, torque can be increased using gearing. Gears slow down the speed of a turn, but they increase its power.

Speaking of power, we usually hear the word *torque* in advertisements for sports cars and pickup trucks, but it's all around us. Consider dancing. Line dances would have to be extremely short (or require extremely long dance floors) if turns weren't built into the choreography. Despite its name, square dancing is built around turns, too. All dancing is, and torque is important to every form. Mostly it comes from pushing off the floor; the harder you push, the faster you spin.

Torque can also be produced by the leg itself. Think of a graceful ballerina effortlessly spinning around and around via fouettés (French for "whipped turning"), rotating many more times than a single push off the ground could account for. By repeatedly extending and retracting her leg, she's creating torque to overcome the rotational inertia of her turns.[6]

Much like dancers gliding across the floor, the reason cars on the highway seem to float so effortlessly from lane to lane with no perceptible turning of their tires is related to what we learned about vectors in Chapter Two. Since at highway speeds the wheels are spinning rapidly, the vector of direction needs to change less with each revolution than it would if the car were moving slowly. And the forces of friction are correspondingly lower with each revolution as well, which is why it's easier to turn the steering wheel of a moving car than a parked one. Again, there's a good business metaphor to ponder.

Lean is another force involved in a turn. Bicyclists lean into turns to avoid being thrown off their bikes. Leaning is a way to overcome the centrifugal force that wants to throw us the other way in a turn—or more properly, the centripetal force that doesn't have a car door to do its dirty work. The bicycle turns because of friction (traction) between the tires and the road, but inertia dictates that the person riding it is going to continue going straight. Only by leaning into the turn can the cyclist overcome that inertia.

And then there's entropy. It may not seem like a force per se, but we see it all around us. In layman's terms, entropy is the tendency for everything in the universe to trend toward disarray. Entropy is why things fall apart; it's why, without countervailing forces, what's whole will go to pieces, what's smooth will grow rough, what works will soon fail, what's profitable today will become unprofitable tomorrow.

We all experience entropy firsthand, every day. Do you ever wonder why, just as things seem to be going well with a project, something happens that causes events to take a turn for the worse? It doesn't necessarily mean you've done anything wrong. Once you understand the principle of entropy—that left to themselves things *always* fall apart—it frees you from always feeling responsible. In fact, perhaps it's your job to hold them together; you can be gravity, metaphorically speaking. That's empowering.

Inertia. Gravity. Momentum. Tension. Friction. Leverage. Torque. Gears. Vectors. Lean. Entropy. Various and competing forces—and force multipliers—that are all involved in turns and turning. You don't have to be a physicist to apply them to any turn your company may be facing, and considering the impact of each can be a useful exercise to help you understand what's really going on. A good example is IndyCar racing.

A race car traveling at high speeds in one direction is going to keep going in that direction unless acted upon with some external force. That's *inertia*.

The car is increasingly harder to stop and easier to turn as it increases its *momentum*.

The car clings to the track rather than flying off into space because of *gravity.* In fact, the cars feature air foils that use oncoming wind to create downforce and counteract the vehicle's tendency to lift off the pavement, effectively increasing the force of gravity.

As the cars race around the turns, banked curves (superelevation) help them rotate around the center of the turn rather than flying off the edge. That's *tension.*

Competing drivers take different "lines" into the turn. An inside line is slower, but shorter. An outside line is faster, but longer. They differ in *leverage.*

Drivers downshift their gears heading into the turn to increase power to the wheels. That's *torque.*

The wheels are spinning so fast it looks like they're not turning, even though the car is. That's because the change in *vector* with each spin of the wheel is so small.

The suspension of the car is tuned just right and its center of gravity kept as low as possible to keep the vehicle as flat as possible and minimize *lean.*

And only the most capable drivers can control a high-powered vehicle around a turn at two hundred miles per hour. If you or I were to do it, it's likely *entropy* would win (and we would definitely lose).

As we can see, every turn is a contest between forces, and they interact in ways that are somewhat predictable. Overcoming inertia is going to involve some tension. Sharper turns require greater lean. Momentum creates leverage. The harder something is to turn, the more friction it will create. Gravity can overcome entropy. These forces play out in myriad ways in everyday situations, and the more we can understand them, the better we'll be able to manage them.

For example, it's impossible to entirely offset centrifugal force by banking a turn, because for any given turn a certain superelevation is just right at only one speed. At all other speeds there will be a force either pulling the car into the center or causing it to skid, which must be offset by friction.

But friction isn't constant under all conditions, either; Daniel Findley reminds us that you also must factor in the weather, "in particular, pavement condition and quality—is it wet, is it icy, is it snowy, is the pavement old, and is friction a problem?" Varying track conditions are why racing teams have all kinds of tires available to them and will often change them in the middle of the race in response to changing weather or wear. As a result of all this, there is rarely a perfect line through a turn.

That goes for any turn—literal or literary. Take the dramatic story arc used in novels and films. Most stories turn on or around the climax, which is where the dramatic tension is at its peak. But there is no singular ideal line through the turn. Some stories begin slowly, focusing on character development, and only gradually increase the pace of the action leading to some sort of climax. Others start with a bang, making you hold onto your seat as the action rapidly unfolds. In every case, however, the use of "dramatic tension" keeps the story turning.

The same is true of music. Mat Langlois points out that in many classical compositions, one musical key is considered the "ruling key," and moving away from that key is interpreted by the listener as a kind of upsetting of the hierarchy that needs resolution. That's what makes music interesting and enables composers to set up melodic narratives.

Langlois says inertia and gravity offer the perfect metaphor for this, because the ruling key exerts a kind of gravitational force holding the piece together. Sections of the piece that depart from the ruling key almost always get pulled back at some point. He says such a "skeleton" underlies most pre-twentieth century classical music, and a similar model can be heard in most of the pop, rock, and folk music we listen to today. "Moving back and forth between tension and resolution, tension and resolution, is a kind of fundamental pattern in Western music," he says. It's also a pattern in business, such as during sensitive negotiations when whatever issues are on the table are discussed, debated, and resolved.

Discordant notes also play a part. "Even a phrase or snippet of music that you and I hear that sounds perfectly nice will usually contain some dissonances," says Langlois. "Otherwise, it sounds completely anodyne." Discordant notes often require some sort of resolution to sound stable again, and the net effect is what we know as harmony. It's a beautiful illustration of how competing forces can combine to create something sublime.

At my firm we have a principle to which we subscribe that simply says, "It's about the idea." We get paid to solve problems, so there can be no compromise as we develop strategic solutions—neither seniority, longevity, rank, nor title matter as we discuss and debate, attempting to get to the core of the issue and identify the best path forward. That often results in a few "discordant notes" being sounded as we work to find a harmonious outcome. It's not easy, but there's no better way to stress test our thinking.

Discord without harmony is a good way to describe the struggle between Union and Confederacy in the Civil War. It featured contests within contests beginning with prewar tension between North and South, abolitionists and slaveowners, Democrats, Whigs, and Republicans. All these forces came to a head in the election of 1860, which elevated Abraham Lincoln to the presidency and provoked the shots at Fort Sumter that rang out shortly thereafter.

Nobody understood what was at stake better than the new president. "I wish it might be more generally and universally understood what the country is now engaged in," Lincoln said. "There is more involved in this contest than is realized by everyone. There is involved in this struggle the question whether your children and my children shall enjoy the privileges we have enjoyed."[7] Part of Lincoln's genius as a leader was his ability to properly frame the context of the moment. The longer and harder a turn is going to be, the more necessary it is to keep people focused on the big picture.

Another necessity is understanding the fundamental human need to know *why*. One of Lincoln's preoccupations during the war—and why his preparation and personality made him precisely the leader the nation needed at that time—was continually working to help his fellow Americans understand the nature of the struggle. "This is essentially a People's contest," he said. "On the side of the Union, it is a struggle for maintaining in the world that form and substance of government whose leading object is to elevate the condition of men . . . to afford all an unfettered start, and a fair chance, in the race of life."[8]

Those are inspiring words, and they elevated the war from a clash of armies to a moral crusade. That would become increasingly important as events continued to unfold.

When the war began, the North had more than twice as many soldiers as the South and much more industrial capacity, including a three-to-one advantage in manpower.[9] It also had a well-established and functioning federal government. But, like the American Revolutionaries some four score years earlier, the South had the advantage of fighting a defensive war in its own territory; in one sense all it had to do was hold out long enough to win.

And it did so with surprising initial success. In 1863, two years into what Northerners thought was going to be a brief contest, British statesman and future prime minister William Gladstone gave the South the advantage, remarking, "Jefferson Davis and the other leaders of the South have made an army; they are making, it appears, a navy; and they have made what is more than either, they have made a nation."[10]

Part of the reason for the South's good performance was the freedom with which Confederate president Davis could operate under the Rebel constitution, which differed in important respects from the U.S. Constitution. Davis could constitutionally only serve one six-year term, which, perhaps as a consequence unanticipated by those who had drafted it, gave him room to make difficult decisions over a longer time frame and without the threat of an election hovering over his head.

There were multiple changes in momentum between North and South throughout the bloody first few years of the war. Derek Frisby says, "From the perspective of the people at that time [in the summer of 1862] you would have had whiplash because you had the Union Army in the west winning at Shiloh, moving deep into the South, and then you had these counter offenses in Virginia that Lee put into place." From those wild swings in 1862 to Union victory at Gettysburg in 1863 to the summer of 1864 when everyone, including Lincoln, seemed to believe the president would lose reelection, constantly shifting momentum would effectively create a stalemate, and many expected the North to seek peace negotiations.

Enter General William Tecumseh Sherman and his "March to the Sea," during which he swiftly and decisively took Atlanta and Savannah and, in large measure, defeated the South's will to fight. Sherman is remembered today for his highly destructive tactics, but early in the war he was most respectful of Southern property, instructing his troops to do as little damage as possible.

The turning point, however, happened when Sherman's army got stuck south of Memphis and was cut off from its supply lines. His troops bravely managed to fight their way out, and as a result Sherman realized if his men could live off the land rather than relying on supply lines it would provide much greater flexibility. This enabled him to seize the initiative and move quickly across the South. Sherman's goal was not to make war on civilians, but by going after their supplies and property he would increasingly deny them the ability to make war and, importantly, damage their morale.

Damage their morale it did, but Sherman's march through the South wasn't the only debilitating factor the Confederates had to deal with on their own turf. Beyond its physical dynamics, one definition of friction is "the clashing between two persons or parties of opposed views."[11] This was happening in spades on both sides of the Mason-Dixon line. Says James McPherson of the South:

> Internal divisions fatally weakened the Confederacy: the state-rights conflict between certain governors and the Richmond government; the disaffection of non-slaveholders from a rich man's war and poor man's fight; libertarian opposition to necessary measures such as conscription and the suspension of habeas corpus; the lukewarm commitment to the Confederacy by quondam Whigs and unionists; the disloyalty of slaves who defected to the enemy whenever they had a chance; growing doubts

> among slaveowners themselves about the justice of their peculiar institution and their cause.[12]

The North was no stranger to internal disputes, either. They began early in the war when the army's significant military advantage didn't deliver a swift and decisive victory. Quite the contrary, as the Union Army suffered a humiliating defeat at the Battle of Bull Run only a few months into Lincoln's presidency. This wasn't some far-off battlefield across the sea. It was within spitting distance of the nation's capital, and the army's humiliating retreat happened in full view of the citizenry.

After the defeat at Bull Run, naysayers in the overconfident North began to emerge immediately and would be a burr under Lincoln's saddle for the duration of the war. Poet Walt Whitman recounted a conversation he overheard from one of the officers returning from defeat, expressing the opinion "that it was useless to fight, that the Southerners had made their title clear, and that the best course for the national government to pursue was to desist from any further attempt at stopping them, and admit them again to the lead, on the best terms they were willing to grant."[13]

To say that there was friction between Lincoln and his generals would be an understatement, particularly with the commander of the Union Army when the war began, George McClellan. Lincoln quickly grew frustrated with McClellan's poor leadership, at one point sending word that he'd like to borrow the Union Army if the general wasn't planning on using it. For his part, McClellan described the president in private correspondence as both an "idiot" and "a well-meaning baboon."[14] When McClellan refused to pursue the retreating Confederate Army after the Battle of Antietam in 1862, Lincoln fired him, only to see his former general run against him in the presidential election of 1864.

Though McClellan would be the first general with whom Lincoln would have a conflict, he was far from the last. After a disastrous attack on Fredericksburg, Lincoln is reported to have cried in the telegraph office as reports came in, muttering, "It's all lost. It's all lost." The president begged the armies in the west to attack the Confederacy at Murfreesboro, Tennessee. But the military leaders there didn't feel prepared and effectively told the commander in chief to take a hike. It's as if they were saying, "Go ahead and fire us, it only looks worse on you," says Derek Frisby.

There were additional internal forces in the North working against one another. Says McPherson, "The North had its large minority alienated by the rich man's war/poor man's fight theme; its outspoken opposition to conscription, taxation, suspension of habeas corpus, and other war measures; its state governors and legislatures and congressmen who tried to thwart administration policies."[15]

This is one of the reasons Lincoln's Republican Party was punished in the congressional elections of 1862. Midterm elections are often referendums on sitting presidents, and this one was particularly biting. By that time Lincoln had done the math and could have pursued a policy of compensated emancipation—paying slaveowners for their slaves and coming out ahead not only in terms of blood but treasure as well. He offered that olive branch to the Southern states and not one took him up on it.

Internal issues on each side of the conflict had as much to do with turns in the war as the battles fought in forest and field. "Northern victory and southern defeat in the war cannot be understood apart from the contingency that hung over every campaign, every battle, every election, every decision during the war," McPherson says.[16] "Defeat causes demoralization and loss of will; victory pumps up morale and the will to win." Ultimately, "The Confederacy succumbed to internal rather than external causes." They "did not lack the means to continue the struggle, but the will to do so."[17]

These competing forces would continue jousting even after the formal end to hostilities, not only across the South but in the halls of Congress, notably with the impeachment of Andrew Johnson, Lincoln's successor.

Interpersonal friction is among the forces at work in almost every human turn—particularly the tendency of people to criticize those making the decisions. Halfway into his third consecutive losing season as the coach of Duke University men's basketball, young Mike Krzyzewski was an unpopular man. But Duke athletic director Tom Butters believed in Krzyzewski and gave him an unsolicited five-year contract extension. Unsurprisingly, many of the school's donors, fans, and even faculty were up in arms. Yet within three years Duke had earned a spot in the Final Four of the NCAA Basketball Tournament, and Krzyzewski went on to win five national championships and more games than any coach in NCAA history.[18]

It would be difficult enough if it were just external second-guessing we had to contend with when faced with a turn; sometimes we're our own worst enemies. One of the destructive internal dynamics my company's research has repeatedly revealed is a lack of alignment among management teams. It may be the most common dysfunction we see—and the most destructive.

If your team is not aligned, it doesn't matter what your strategy is—it won't get executed. Worse, lack of internal alignment can often go unnoticed or be willfully ignored. It's easy to miss someone rolling their eyes, to excuse perennial lateness to meetings, to ignore whispers in the hallway. But we neglect this behavior at our peril.

I recall one instance where internal alignment was the problem, but ignoring it was impossible. I was leading a retreat in the impressive offices of a Manhattan skyscraper, where the sales and management team of a notable financial services firm had gathered to confront the company's declining market share. The sales team was complaining that competitors were undercutting their prices and there was no way they could close enough deals without some margin relief. On the other side of the table the management team insisted that, as a premium brand, the company couldn't cut its prices without taking an unacceptable hit to its perception in the marketplace, so the sales team should just "sell harder."

This was our first meeting, where in most cases everyone around the table is polite and deferential to one another as the discussion gets going. Imagine the look on my face when ten minutes in the two sides were yelling and screaming, hurling F-bombs at each other. "At least they don't have a problem with passive aggression here," I mused to myself.

Though it's not usually quite so expressive, internal disagreements are a reality in every corporation. Once when I was sharing our research regarding this issue, a hand went up in the back of the room. I paused for a moment as the questioner asked, "I'm a sole proprietor—is it possible for me to have a lack of management alignment?" He was joking—sort of—but my answer was clear: absolutely. If you've ever been of two minds about a decision you need to make, that qualifies.

We all have that little voice in our head that calls into question our ability and decisions; at the time of his contract extension, Mike Krzyzewski himself was expecting to be fired. Our self-doubt may have a point, and it's something we shouldn't ignore. But we have a choice whether to reflexively submit to our inner critic or recognize that it's just one of the forces at work with which we must contend.

We tend to think of the various forces involved in a turn as primarily external—a competitor that opposes us, an economy that holds us back, or a technological innovation that threatens to shake up how we do business. But time and again we must also contend with the enemy within, whether it's the inertia of resistance to change, the tension of conflicting opinions, or the friction of hurt feelings. These are all real and powerful forces that can be counteracted if and as we lean in, look for leverage, and gear up; we can bring the weight of gravity and the power of momentum to our effort to overcome entropy. There's rarely a foregone conclusion.

The outcome of the Reformation was certainly not certain—far from it. "Protestantism was born in conflict, not only with the rest of the world, but with itself,"[19] says Alec Ryrie, noting that two Dutch friars were the first to be burned at the stake as heretics in Luther's time, in 1523. Before the sixteenth century was over, more than three thousand others would be condemned to death not for anything they had done, but simply for what they believed.[20]

Luther, as we know, was not one of them. In his case the pen was mightier than the sword—or stake. Like Sherman's march through the South, the invention of gunpowder in late medieval times, or the machine guns that debuted in the 1898 Battle of Omdurman (which a young witness, Winston Churchill, described as "death by machinery"[21]), writing in the common tongue and having his thoughts multiplied by the printing press were forces Luther's foes had never before faced.

Says Ryrie:

> In 1518, Luther discovered that he could write: accessibly, pungently, mixing soaring ecstasies with brutal street fighting. He had a knack for unforgettable images and analogies and a sense of paradox that made his arguments seem almost irrefutable. He could do it in Latin, like a good scholar, but he could also do it wonderfully in German, seizing his readers by the throat and pulling them into the debate. . . . Orthodoxy's defenders were entirely unprepared for the storm of print that had engulfed them.[22]

Although the printing press had by that time been around longer than Luther himself, he was the first to master its use for public consumption. In 1523, nearly four hundred separate editions of his pamphlets were published, incredible output for just one man. "Luther's books changed the rules of religious debate, which was meant to be a game for educated elites, played in universities in the decent obscurity of Latin," says Ryrie. "Luther flung open the gates. Now anyone who could read German, or who knew someone who could read German, could join in."[23]

And join in they did. That particular "moment" of the Reformation bred a host of other forces that fed off each other and fueled the fire, says Megan Armstrong. "I think of the forces as kind of taking on a life of their own and multiplying. . . . A lot of his criticisms were not new, but he has the technology of the printing press, and mercantile support, and political support to be able to rapidly spread these ideas. . . . It was a transformative time." This was also the moment German nationalism was developing, less to do with borders than language, and Luther's adept use of publishing gave him undue influence.

The Reformation began to spread not through pitched battles but through the written word, including the widespread influence of catechisms—religious instruction manuals usually taking the form of a series of questions and answers—even among the priesthood. The catechisms of the 1740s–1780s—in particular the Heidelberg Catechism of 1563 that united various Protestant factions by leaving unaddressed the controversial topic of predestination—acted as significant accelerants of reformed theology.[24]

Speaking of factions, Luther himself was quickly outflanked by more radical reformers. Just five years after making his bold stand, there was a significant uprising in the surrounding environs by which peasants organized amateur armies to go to war against their feudal lords, using religious arguments to demand additional rights and freedoms. Luther condemned the brief but bloody "Peasant War," which he arguably inspired and in which one hundred thousand people from the surrounding towns and villages were killed.

In the dance between politics and religion, the Reformation was a struggle for the backing of secular governments. Says Ryrie, "Without their support, no religious dissidents could last for long. With it, the old church was at their mercy."[25] In Germany, this played out in a variety of ways in a variety of regions, the most significant being the protective hand the Duke of Saxony held over Luther, paving the way for other fiefdoms throughout

Eastern and Northern Europe to determine their own religious fates. In France, various rulers were less rebellious of Rome, but in England, the fireworks were just beginning to start.

The infamous Henry VIII saw the emergence of Protestantism as a way of throwing off the yoke of Rome so that he could not only claim supremacy over the English church but also justify the illegitimate annulment of his first marriage, which the pope had refused to grant, and subsequent second marriage to Anne Boleyn, whom he would later behead for accusations of adultery and incest, likely fabricated.

To further justify his behavior, Henry required every man in the kingdom to swear an oath recognizing both his marriage and his sovereignty over the Church of England. In 1539 he also legalized the English Bible and made it available to some nine thousand parishes throughout the country, "because of his touchingly naïve belief that anyone else who read the Bible would discover in it what he had discovered himself—the doctrine of the Royal Supremacy," says Ryrie. "No matter: for evangelicals, a freely available Bible was almost the sum of all their dreams."[26]

But it was not to last. After Henry met his maker in 1547, his nine-year-old son, Edward VI, succeeded him but died after a short six-year reign. His daughter Mary then inherited the throne, violently turning the nation back toward Catholicism and burning some three hundred Protestant men and women at the stake. She ruled for only five years before her untimely death, which for the Reformation in England was about as timely as it gets. John Craig believes that had Mary lived longer, her ruthless persecution may have snuffed out the still-nascent movement. As it was, says Craig, "those [three hundred] deaths acted as an accelerant to the movement and reinforced sympathy towards the Protestants." Following Mary's death, her devout half-sister, Elizabeth, became queen and once again turned to Protestantism as the state religion, maintaining a steady hand on the throne for the next forty-five years.

These forces and counter forces were in contest throughout Europe for two centuries following the turn Luther initiated in 1517. And they were as prevalent within the Catholic Church as outside of it. Megan Armstrong says that reformers loyal to the church believed that "resistance alone [to Protestantism] is not working . . . if we want to respond then we need to think creatively and imaginatively and honestly and work forward."

This is a helpful way of looking at a turn not of your own choosing. Sometimes circumstances are forced upon us, and our choice is to either deny and resist them or embrace them to our advantage. Resistance may feel brave, but it is often futile. It's often better to accept the new conditions on the ground and determine what best to do about them.

For nearly two decades beginning in 1545, the Council of Trent met in northern Italy to do just that. Says Ryrie of the council, "It decisively rejected Protestant doctrines and laid out an ambitious vision for disciplinary reform and educational renewal of the church which was implemented with verve by a reinvigorated papacy and by a series of religious orders. Over the next century, a more disciplined, better educated Catholicism took shape, depriving the Protestants of some of their best talking points."[27] This "Counter Reformation" breathed new life into the Catholic Church, and oddly enough, into Protestantism as well. "The Protestant and Catholic Reformations accelerated each other," says Armstrong.

By the time Luther's moment was complete (though not the "moment" of the Reformation, as we've seen), he ended up less a radical than a mediating influence. Says Ryrie, "For those princes, city councils, and people who had imbibed the reformers' preaching, going back to the pre-1517 world was hard to imagine. So, Luther found himself representing a safe middle way, the acceptable face of reform. It was an outcome that neither he nor anyone else had expected. His reformation neither transformed the church nor was crushed by it."[28]

Thus, to the principle "turns beget other turns" we can add "forces affect other forces." Just as the Peasants' War reflected the increasing illegitimacy of the feudal system, the enterprising printers who embraced the leading edge of technology at the time made their fortunes courtesy of Martin Luther. Before his prolific contributions, the printing press was essentially an industrial tool used to produce dense texts for limited interests, much as the internet in its early days was used for narrow collaboration among science and engineering professionals. Once Luther's works had demonstrated the power of the press, however, there was no turning back.

Still, the turn from feudalism to capitalism was neither quick nor direct. A transitionary form of public-private partnership known as mercantilism temporarily balanced the tension between government force and economic freedom. In mercantilism, a term derived from the Italian word for "merchant," corporations and governments allied themselves to broaden the reach and increase the treasure of both, most notably of precious metals but also of exotic items from faraway places such as spices and silk. Mercantilism worked in different ways in different countries, but its premise was always based on government managing the economy to enhance state wealth and power.

Because these were the days before Adam Smith's insight that wealth is a function of products and services more than gold and silver, government assumed a bigger role in the economy. Mercantilists believed that the regime's power should be used to stimulate the output of goods, limit domestic consumption, levy tariffs on imports, and try to create a favorable balance of trade by which a country would export more than it imports. That would in turn increase the nation's stores of gold and silver, which could be used to strengthen the army.

Whereas in a feudal economy land was wealth, under mercantilism wealth became much more portable in the form of goods and precious metals. Given the you-scratch-my-back-I'll-scratch-yours nature of their relationship with corporations, governments were more than happy to protect those who did their mercantilist bidding.

The most notable—some would say notorious—example of mercantilism was the British East India Company, which historian William Dalrymple labeled the "original corporate raiders." Formed in 1599 to trade with India and Southeast Asia, the corporation received a British Royal Charter from Queen Elizabeth (yes, the Protestant reformer Queen Elizabeth) in 1600. The queen herself was a shareholder in the company, which, without firing a shot (officially, at least), became the tip of the spear of British imperialism.

But mercantilist economies succeed only as long as governments effectively control the monopolies they spawn and keep an artificial lid on prices and wages, which they are notoriously bad at doing. In the heyday of mercantilist Europe, a continued influx of gold and silver led to inflation, which rose faster than wages, and zero-sum protectionist policies between increasingly powerful nation-states often led to war.

Mercantilism can most charitably be thought of as a transitionary system that acted as a sort of training wheels for market capitalism. It has not disappeared entirely, as tempting as it is to centralized governments, but neither has free market capitalism existed in pure form. Generally speaking, however, the past four centuries have demonstrated that the freer those in the private sector are to pursue their own economic interests, the more prosperous the economy will become and the more peaceful relations between nations will be, as Smith predicted.

This is something Ronald Reagan knew in his bones, which is why he was so confident the West would emerge from the Cold War victorious. "Would you like to hear my theory of the Cold War?" he asked an aide before he became president. "Some people think I'm simplistic," he said. "But there's a difference between being simple and being simplistic. My theory about the Cold War is that we win, and they lose."[29]

The win/lose paradigm is indeed reflective of certain strategic situations such as war, politics, and sports, because the conditions in which those contests take place are bounded by limits: limited geography in the case of war, limited elective offices in the case of politics, limited time, distance, or at-bats in the case of sports. But that's not the case in market economies.

In a free market, competitive dynamics are always temporary, and each player has the ability to turn them around. If a company makes, say, wallpaper, and one of its competitors corners the market on raw materials, it has a big problem. But those who run the company can choose not to be defeated: they have technical know-how, manufacturing capacity, a distribution network, R&D capabilities, access to capital, customer knowledge, and, most importantly, lessons they may have learned that can apply to their turnaround. George Gilder underscores how even in loss there is learning, saying, "Capitalism accumulates the capital gains not only of its successes but also of its failures, capitalized in new knowledge."[30]

Market economics enables us—in fact, requires us—to not confuse commerce with conflict. Believing the only way to win is by crushing your opponent is likely to lead to a kind of brutal commoditization that causes everyone to lose. There is only one Bull Run, one available seat in your congressional district, and only one World Series champion, but in business there can be unlimited winners. In war, the tables turning on you could be deadly; in a restaurant, it means you're doing something right.

Turning the tables was very much on the mind of Doug Pruitt and Richard Condit as they tried to balance the forces pelting Sundt from all directions. They had observed that the best performing companies were able to address the future without compromising success in the present. To do so they had to be adept at creating and managing change. "Too much organizational consistency turns a company into a bureaucratic nightmare and stifles innovation," says Condit. "Too much operational flexibility creates confusion, inefficiencies, and silos."[31]

The two had to figure out a way to balance those conflicting forces. "We wanted organizational consistency around the company vision, mission, core values, and the key bridging strategies that would get us to our ideal future state," says Pruitt. "However, the specific tactics that profit and service centers would use to achieve those strategies were left to those organizations to figure out."[32]

The ongoing struggle at Sundt was between a past that was proven and a future yet unseen. That may sound unusual, but it's the case in all our turns. The road behind us is behind us precisely because we've successfully traversed it, but no one can see around the next curve. It's important to remain cognizant of all the forces at work and maintain our center of gravity as we plot our course.

Says Pruitt, "We sold land. We sold two small companies that were losing money. I shut down two divisions. We had too much overhead. And I changed the management out entirely in one division." That created a significant drop in morale. Pruitt spent a lot of what he calls "seat time" with his people, visiting various offices, telling them what was happening and why, and showing them the numbers to prove it. "We were trying to instill the fact that yep, we're in business, we're a great company, we've got a great history, and we're going to be great," he told his people. "But you've got to hang in there. And you've got to do your part."

At one point when Sundt was selling 60 percent of its construction equipment, someone in the highway division told Pruitt, "If you do that, Doug, we're gonna go broke." His response? "Well let's look at it a different way. We're going broke anyway so we might as well try something different."

One of those different things in Sundt's struggle with the past was the need to overcome a natural loss of nerve and make significant investments in the future when that future was looking bleaker every day. At that time, all of the company's vital information had been housed in a centralized data processing center using outdated technology, a risk the company could no longer bear that was, in Pruitt's words, "like a boat anchor."[33] The company began investing in technology that would significantly enhance its estimating, project scheduling, contract management, and customer relationship management capabilities, enabling it to achieve big gains in both quality and productivity. "The bottom line is that you must be willing to invest," says Pruitt. "Instead of asking whether you can afford to invest, ask if your company can afford not to."[34]

The combination of inertia and entropy can be deadly. Without Pruitt's relentless efforts to overcome the obstacles taking his company down, Sundt would have become a footnote like so many other failed corporations. Instead, he stepped into the change and harnessed its forces to turn the company right side up. It's an oft-repeated model that leads to unexpected and often unprecedented results.

The world of sports offers many examples of how, rather than resisting a turn, a willingness to embrace it can provide a competitive edge. In 1966, Coach Don Haskins shocked the college basketball world when his Texas Western (now the University of Texas El Paso) Miners, featuring the first all-black starting lineup, defeated the storied Kentucky Wildcats for the national championship. Only two years after the passing of the Civil Rights Act, it demonstrated the real-world benefits of equal opportunity and added momentum to the turn that had begun when Jackie Robinson broke the color barrier in Major League Baseball in 1947.

Three years after the Miners' improbable win, "Broadway Joe" Namath guaranteed a victory in the Super Bowl for the upstart New York Jets, a member of the American Football League that until that point had been considered a weakling compared to the fierce and fearsome National Football League with which it had recently merged. It was a turn that accelerated the growth of the world's most profitable sports league, today's NFL.[35]

And eleven years after Namath's bold prediction, Herb Brooks used an unorthodox recruiting strategy and frenetic style of play to lead a U.S. Olympic hockey team comprised of amateur college kids past the intimidating and heretofore invincible professionals of the Soviet Union and on to an Olympic gold medal. The victory represented a sea change in American psychology just as recently elevated Pope John Paul II, new British Prime Minister Margaret Thatcher, and a soon-to-be elected President Ronald Reagan would change economic and political history by hastening the collapse of the Soviet Union.

These examples all demonstrate the principle that if you want to make something turn it's your job to disrupt the existing order and set the contest in motion. Don't be surprised to hear a yelp from those whose equilibrium you're upsetting, and don't be taken aback if you're tempted to yelp yourself. A lack of control is always disconcerting.

When I was young, a handful of older kids on our swim team bound my hands and feet with giant rubber bands and threw me into the pool. I don't think they would have let me drown, but I wasn't about to find out. I was a good enough swimmer not to panic, and I understood that if I fought the water it would take me down; flailing is the first step in drowning. I also knew I could use the water's resistance to my advantage and rise to the surface. With a bit of effort and a calm demeanor, I was able to escape my bonds, and that day I learned a valuable lesson: the difference between sinking and swimming can depend on whether you view the water as friend or foe. That which can take you down might also lift you up.

And that which threatens you can be your salvation. For nearly four days in the spring of 1970, the world held its breath as the fate of three American astronauts hung in the balance following an oxygen tank explosion two hundred thousand miles from earth. "Houston, we have a problem," Apollo 13 commander Jim Lovell calmly reported in a radio transmission, in what might have been the understatement of the year.

With the command module severely damaged, the crew took refuge in the lunar module and worked with Mission Control to try and find a safe passage back to earth. In a bold and brilliant move, Houston guided the crew through instructions that would enable them to use the lunar module's descent engine to redirect the ship's trajectory around the moon, using lunar gravity to slingshot them back to earth. Amazingly, it worked, and in an odd turn of events the failed mission enhanced NASA's reputation as never before.[36] Isaac Newton would have been as pleased as he was stunned to see it.

The lesson of Apollo 13 applies to other avenues of life. "Investments are in fact purposeful experiments, and whatever the outcome, the results are informative," says Gilder of the benefits of entrepreneurial endeavor. "Even the failures in a sense succeed and the much-remarked 'waste' of the system is often redeemed by the accumulation of information and experience, a crucial form of intangible capital, held by both the entrepreneurs themselves and by the society at large."[37]

We see this reflected in the theater as well. Playwright David Mamet says that as a good drama moves through its arc, "each character has a swell idea of how to get what he wants. The scene ends when and because he was proved wrong and must, now, start again, balked of his desires, but with the new information gained in his momentary failure."[38]

The key word there is *momentary*, as failure is sometimes success in disguise. Had Luther not been accused of being a heretic and brought before the Diet of Worms, his ninety-five theses may have been lost to the wind. Had Sherman's army not been forced to survive without its supply lines, his sweeping victory across the South would never have happened. Had Doug Pruitt not been kept in the dark about the condition of his company prior to being named CEO, he may never have taken the job. And had my company not gone through a near-death experience, it wouldn't have developed the expertise to help stalled, stuck, and stale organizations turn themselves around.

In any arena, turns are moments of opportunity. Without turns, entropy would cause us to drift from everything that has order and makes sense. But just as the torque of a wrist helps tighten a screw, the friction of the wood resists it. Just as the potter's wheel makes clay more malleable, the knife on the sharpener can create sparks. There are multiple forces at work in every turn—some that work for it, and some against it.

The good news is that you and I are among those forces. In nature, the forces of tension and friction and torque simply do what they do. In business, we can use tension and friction and torque—and traction and leverage and momentum and every other force—to create the conditions necessary for success.

We can push ourselves through a turn, just as the tires on a car use friction to push it toward the center of a curve, or a melodic narrative seems to effortlessly move a musical composition along. The printing press and the birth pangs of the separation of secular governments from papal rule moved the Reformation along in ways Luther could never have foreseen. Lincoln's repeated appeals to our nation's founding principles and bold issuance of the Emancipation Proclamation so gripped the hearts of his countrymen that they were determined to see the nation's bloodiest conflict through to its end. Don Haskins's determination to put the best players on the court regardless of the color of their skin made the rapid integration of college basketball inevitable.

We can pull ourselves through a turn, the way tension on the string of a yo-yo snaps it back into our hands or a novel's unresolved story line keeps us engrossed. Mercantilism could not survive the inescapable market forces that mediate power once concentrated in the hands of parliament or politburo. Joe Namath's reckless guarantee of a victory turned out to be prescient when it motivated his teammates to go above and beyond to win. And the tension at Mission Control resulted in intense focus and concentration that kept the Apollo 13 crew alive as it lassoed the moon.

Here's an interesting exercise. Get a few of your people in front of a whiteboard and document the various forces and their parallels in your current situation. How would you characterize the inertia of your company and industry? What are the forces of entropy? How does what you do act as gravity, and what are the vital forces holding it all together? Where is the momentum—internally, among your products and services, or externally in the marketplace?

What points of tension are you dealing with, or avoiding? Where are you experiencing friction—positive, that's propelling you forward, and negative, that's holding you back? What points of leverage are you using, or missing? What would it mean to increase your torque, or gear up? Where should you be leaning in more?

The answers to these questions may vary depending on who you have in the room or when you're doing the exercise. Some may come easily, and others might require more thinking. But I suspect every aspect of your operations and marketing can be described using the metaphor of the physical forces in a turn. Sometimes stepping out of reality and into allegory can reveal things you haven't yet seen.

Every turn is the result of conflicting forces. No business will ever be free from opposing ideas, competing organizations, new developments, and even its own pride and prejudices and internal contradictions. Those of us in leadership can thus never take the success of a turn for granted. But neither do we need to resign ourselves to a predetermined result. We play a significant role in the outcome.

> ***The Principle of the Contest***
> *Every turn is a contest of competing forces. You are one of them.*

CHANGES

"I turn to stone."
Electric Light Orchestra

When Don Haskins lined up his Texas Western Miners against the Kentucky Wildcats for the 1966 NCAA basketball championship, he didn't have anything other than winning on his mind. "I wasn't out to be a pioneer when we played Kentucky," he said. "I was simply playing the best players on the team, and they happened to be black."[1]

Dana Hunsinger Benbow, a sportswriter for the *Indianapolis Star*, noted that it was only one year before that historic game that the "Bloody Sunday" march from Selma to Montgomery took place. It was fewer than three years prior to the game that President Johnson ordered the National Guard to end Governor George Wallace's blockade preventing black students from enrolling at the University of Alabama and Martin Luther King stood on the steps of the Lincoln Memorial to give his "I Have a Dream" speech.[2] More than a full century after the end of the Civil War, change had been slow in coming.

But following the turn of events at the Cole Field House in College Park, Maryland, intercollegiate sports would never be the same. "That game was the catalyst that opened athletic, academic, and employment doors for those who followed us," said Harry Flournoy, a member of the Texas Western team. "No longer would we be kept out of mainstream America." "Without question," says the NCAA's Derrick Gragg, "it was one of the most significant, impactful college sporting events in the history of our country."[3]

Three months following the 1966 NCAA basketball tournament came another significant turn in sports, this time in football. On June 8 of that year, the National Football League announced a merger with its upstart rival, the American Football League, to form the modern NFL. At the end of that season, the first Super Bowl pitted a team from each of the former leagues against one another. Unsurprisingly, the then-dominant NFC trounced the AFC by an average of more than twenty points in the first two Super Bowls.

In 1969, however, when "Broadway Joe" Namath guaranteed and subsequently delivered a victory for his New York Jets against the heavily favored Baltimore Colts, it marked the first time a former AFL team would win a Super Bowl. And it broadened the appeal of professional football as never before. Both attendance and TV viewership soared, and when ABC launched what would become a perennial TV-ratings juggernaut, *Monday Night Football*, two years later, the network tipped its hat to Namath and the Jets by making sure they were on the field for the first game. Alas, the Jets lost that matchup.

Neither Haskins nor Namath could have conceived of the changes their victories would lead to; they simply wanted to win. But both instances demonstrate how a single turn of events can alter things. Whenever we find ourselves facing a turn—whether initiated by us or not of our own choosing—change is about to happen.

Look up *turn* in the dictionary and you'll find several dozen definitions, many of them associated with dramatic change. You might turn your head away from something you don't want to see. You might turn from a life of drugs or crime. You might turn on a light so you can read better or turn it off so you can go to sleep. But not all turns are up or down, on or off, or 180 degrees.

True, a competitive swimmer heads as fast as possible in one direction before quickly flipping to head in the opposite direction, and a gymnast who gets to the end of a balance beam has no option but to turn around and begin working the other way. But transatlantic flights follow gentle arcs around the earth, road cyclists might navigate dozens of curves without ever fully turning around, and lazy rivers meander their way to the sea. When Robert Frost took the road less traveled by, the reason it made all the difference was not because he turned around but because he chose one path instead of another. No matter their degree, however, turns always bring change.

One of the joys of working with struggling organizations is their willingness to consider new ideas; nothing will make you open to surgery more than pain. Because companies in decline are acutely aware of the disadvantaged situation in which they find themselves—whether it's industry commoditization, shifts in the competitive landscape, tardiness to technological advancements, or any one of dozens of other reasons—they're more open to taking calculated risks. Pain has a way of focusing their minds on seeking transformative solutions.

Sometimes those solutions involve new product development, where it pays to identify the pain points of their customers; seeking innovation in frustration is an evergreen method of creating change. At my company we nurture our capability to develop new ideas in a fun way by maintaining a "What

Doesn't Work" wall. We encourage our staff to post annoyances small and large on the wall as a way of coping with their own everyday irritations. Items on the wall range from titanic frustrations like the U.S. health care system to minor annoyances such as unstable cocktail tables, no-show socks that roll up in your shoes, and wet coasters that stick to the bottom of your glass. Solve any of those and you'll turn frustration into delight. And possibly make a lot of money.

It's fun to consider what doesn't work in general, but if you turn the attention to your own industry, you're likely to come up with a host of potential innovations. It's not always easy to see what's right in front of you, since your staff and customers are likely to have developed work-arounds and/or tolerance for those things that make them almost unnoticeable. But there's always something that doesn't work—or doesn't work well—and envisioning what needs to change is a way of determining which way the road should turn, effectively putting your company in the driver's seat regarding the future of your industry.

In auto racing, changes in direction often determine changes in outcomes. Drag races happen only on straightaways, of course, and they offer their own thrills as they demonstrate the power of pure acceleration (and cool parachutes that bring the dragsters to a gentle stop). But the most popular forms of auto racing—NASCAR, IndyCar, Formula 1—involve turns of some kind. Turns not only enable spectators to follow the action by keeping the tracks self-contained, they make the contests themselves much more interesting.

"Managing change" is a good way to describe what a driver must do to win in the turns. The strategies for doing so vary depending upon whether the car is in the lead or behind, taking the turn alone or as part of a group, or what the weather conditions, track conditions, and the condition of the car's tires may be.

The parallels to turns in business are obvious; it's why "change management" is a billion-dollar industry. Each of us is the "driver" of change in our own companies. Sometimes the task is to stay ahead, while other times we must come from behind, and we're all faced with ever-evolving conditions. Some races we win, some we lose. With each turn, however, the trajectory in which we've been heading comes to an end and a new one begins.

The shape (degree) of the turn is the first factor a race car driver must consider. On most IndyCar and NASCAR tracks, the curves are predictable and always the same: 180-degrees, banked in such a way that they help keep the cars' tires on the asphalt. On other tracks, and on surface streets where Formula 1 races take place, the turn can be anything from a quick and simple corner to a death-defying hairpin.

Whatever the case, drivers attempt to identify the ideal "line" through each turn, effectively trying to straighten it out so that they can carry as much speed into and through the turn as possible. The line will vary not only by the type of turn, but by all the conditions mentioned above as well as the driver's skill and the car's horsepower.

In every curve there's an apex, which is the pivotal point of the line taken through it. The apex is typically the sharpest and most dangerous part of a turn where car and driver attempt to overcome peak centrifugal forces. If the drivers go too slow through the apex, they risk getting passed; if they go too fast, they risk drifting up the curve and into the wall—and perhaps into another car or two along the way.

Unless drifting is part of their strategy, which in some races it is. A drift happens when the speed of a car overcomes the friction between its tires and the track, either because the turn is unusually sharp, or the car is moving too fast. While it may look as if the cars are sliding out of control, the drivers know what they're doing, turning the steering wheel in the opposite direction of the curve (counter-steering) to create friction in the opposite direction.

The drivers may not fully understand the physics behind what they're doing, but the combination of instinct, training, and experience gets them through the turn time after time and is just one more dimension of the competition. You may have experienced drifting when driving in snow or ice yourself, instinctively counter-steering to get back into your lane. That's a lot less fun than drivers have on the track, but just as exhilarating.

All of this is what makes professional drivers professionals. Navigating turns at high speed takes a great deal of instinct, expertise, and nerve. They must choose the right line, know when to downshift, determine the correct time and amount to brake, and choose the precise moment just past the apex when they can begin accelerating and preparing for the next corner, all in the space of a few seconds. That sounds like the agenda of an interesting management conference to me.

Some changes that result from turns take much longer to reveal themselves than they do in a high-banked corner or harrowing hairpin. As the Reformation progressed and everyday people were increasingly able to read and interpret the scriptures themselves, the role and nature of the clergy slowly changed. In the new world of Protestantism, pastors replaced priests and were free to marry. New institutions of higher learning developed and expanded, loosening the grip of Rome on theological education. And state power, which for so long had been allied with the church, was in many cases now replacing it.

By the mid-1500s, *cuius regio, eius religio* ("whose realm, their religion") became the norm across much of Europe. This meant local rulers could effectively dictate the religion of their subjects, rather than everyone taking their cues from Rome. Their edicts may have arisen from sincere belief, or the rulers may have acted from expedience, publicly displaying their independence from Rome or proclaiming their allegiance to it. But no longer was the Catholic Church the church of all Europe, and the idea began to emerge that church and state occupy separate realms—an idea we take for granted in the modern West that was completely foreign at the time. As Megan Armstrong put it, "Once they unleash the possibilities for change—of conscience, and what constitutes piety and truth—when that starts to be opened up for questions, it's very hard for authority figures to put it back in the box."

This is important to keep in mind when initiating a turn—it can't be undone. If you and your team come to a fork in the road, arrive at a dead end, or simply find the direction in which things are heading unhealthy or unproductive, a turn may in fact be what's called for. Just don't assume you can fully control it, and don't expect you can go back. The world will have already changed.

A handful of times over the course of running my company, I've had employees come to me and confess they're considering a different career or a new job they've been offered. I've been honored that they have brought the situation to me rather than just submitting their resignation; I consider it a reflection of the healthy corporate culture we've worked hard to establish. Inevitably, however, as we discuss the pluses and minuses of their new opportunity vs. their current position, the possibility of their being able to return arises. As much as I've wanted to tell them the door is always open, in truth it's not. No one can say where the company will be if and when they want to come back, or if there will be an open position, or even if they'll still be a good fit. They'll change and we'll change, no matter how brief the time is that they're away. Change itself has its consequences.

In Reformation England, the 1534 Act of Supremacy gave the Crown authority over the church, which no longer recognized the primacy of the pope. But King Henry VIII also promoted the newly printed English Bible, and its widespread and popular embrace led to an aggressive form of Protestantism that would come back to bite the Crown hard. "It might look as though the state has, over the course of the sixteenth century, put the church firmly in its place," says historian John Craig, "but it has done so in a way that actually releases religious beliefs that only a Protestant monarch is acceptable for the British Isles." That's some change, and one that Martin Luther could never have anticipated a century prior.

This is why Alec Ryrie believes the Reformation was a political turn as much as a religious one. Of those shifting tectonics he says, "The tremors can, ultimately, be traced back to Luther's rejection of every authority beyond the believer's conscience bound by scripture. Obedience was a Christian virtue, but who exactly should Protestants obey? A godly Prince? A tyrant? A preacher—and if so, which one? In the end, only their own consciences, before God and informed by scripture, could answer that question."[4]

It also opened the door, however slightly at first, to political participation by the masses, who up until this point had largely been mere subjects of a regime. "It was the first time," Ryrie says, "the English (male) population as a whole had ever been formally drawn into politics."[5] Further,

> These ideals, which seem natural to our own age, are in the span of human history very unusual indeed. That we should all have a say in choosing our own rulers and that those rulers' powers over us should be limited—these principles are in obvious tension, as every society that has tried to combine liberty and democracy has discovered. Without Protestantism and its peculiar preoccupations, that strange and marvelous synthesis could never have come into being as it has.[6]

In addition to religious and political change, the Reformation brought about significant cultural change, specifically in the realm of individualism, another ideal we take for granted today that was unheard of in earlier times. "'Here I stand, I can do no other' is very familiar to us today," says Megan Armstrong of Martin Luther's famous confession at the Diet of Worms. "It was totally foreign back then."

Armstrong is quick to point out that, in Luther's mind, following one's conscience wasn't about having the right to your own opinion but rather about understanding shared truth. Luther didn't believe, as is so common today, that everyone had their own truth—far from it—but simply that everyone could discover and was responsible to God's truth. Nevertheless, the change had been set in motion, and it should be unsurprising that Luther's at-the-time radical theology would have downstream effects in every realm of life.

Historian and philosopher of science Steve Fuller described the sensibility of the late Reformation scientists as one informed by their reading the Bible themselves, something unheard of among their predecessors. Their worldview, he suggests, was, "We should aspire to understand all of nature by proposing bold hypotheses (something of which we are capable because of the *imago dei*) but to expect and admit error (something to which we are inclined to because of the *peccatum originis*) whenever we fall short in light of the evidence."[7]

That's about as good a characterization of the scientific method as there is, and the pioneers of the Scientific Revolution (Newton, Copernicus, Galileo, and others) took it upon themselves to discover the fingerprints of God in every aspect of creation. They were not alone, as that line of thinking trickled down even to those who pursued more practical occupations.

One of the manifestations of this mindset in the first decades following the Reformation was the rapid growth of the timekeeping business. Between 1500 and 1700, the vast majority of clockmakers in the swiftly growing industry were Protestants, as "the clock mechanism took on a quasi-divine aspect in many sixteenth-century eyes," according to Robin Barnes, a professor of history at Davidson College. "It became a metaphor both for the entire cosmos and for the ideal working of the human world."[8]

The first rudimentary timekeeping devices date back to ancient Egypt. Evidence of different versions of sundials, hourglasses, and "timesticks" have been found throughout Europe and Asia as well, but it wasn't until the fourteenth century that true mechanical clocks emerged.[9] Throughout history, people all over the world had been interested in tracking time, but something happened during the Reformation to accelerate interest in clocks as never before. Barnes calls it "the personalization of time" and suggests it reflected a "trend to individual self-examination and constant personal discipline that emerged forcefully in late sixteenth- and early seventeenth-century Puritanism."[10]

And led to the Protestant work ethic, a term so rooted in our culture that we hardly give it a second thought. Today, preoccupation with time is so embedded in our minds that we naturally think of turns happening in a clockwise (which we view as moving forward) or counterclockwise (which we easily interpret as being counterproductive) direction. We intuitively believe that if we're going with the clock, it's a good thing, while going against it—or even stopping for a moment to rest—is problematic.

There's a reason for this. The incessant pace of change is something with which our forebears never had to deal—at least not to the extent we do today. Changes that in those days took years or sometimes decades to cascade into other realms of life may take only an instant in ours. Information, as a non-material thing, has always been "frictionless," but its movement was historically constrained by material beings who could travel only at the speed of a horse or ship; today it zips around the world at the speed of light.

That puts incredible pressure on us to continually reevaluate how we think and what we do. Our modern economy is filled with drama that our forebears never knew. But not all drama is the same, and not every turn follows the same arc. Unlike when we are navigating a curve in the road, there is no single best line through the turns of commerce.

In *Toward a Science of Human Stories*, a team of researchers from the University of Vermont analyzed more than four thousand novels and found six primary dramatic turns stories tend to take.[11] Novelist Joe Bunting then took those turns and illustrated them using notable examples:

Rags to Riches (rise): A continuous upward turn towards a happy ending, such as in Jane Austen's *Pride and Prejudice* or George Bernard Shaw's *Pygmalion* (popularized in the film *My Fair Lady*).

Riches to Rags (fall): A turn from good to bad. Examples include George Orwell's *Animal Farm*, Joseph Heller's *Catch 22* and the ultimate tear-jerker for any woman that's had a baby boy, Robert Munsch's *Love You Forever*.

Man in a Hole (fall-rise): A popular arc represented in books like J.R.R. Tolkien's *The Hobbit* and Lewis Carroll's *Alice in Wonderland*.

Icarus (rise-fall): Named for the Greek myth about a boy who flies too close to the sun, this is a common arc found in Shakespeare's *Macbeth*, Ernest Hemingway's *The Old Man and the Sea*, Michael Crichton's *Jurassic Park*, F. Scott Fitzgerald's *The Great Gatsby*, and Susan Collins's *The Hunger Games*.

Cinderella (rise-fall-rise): Disney may not have invented this sequence of turns, but has increasingly perfected it, from *Cinderella* to *Pinocchio* to *Aladdin* to *Frozen* to *Up*.

Oedipus (fall-rise-fall): Many tragic story arcs follow this trajectory, including Shakespeare's *Hamlet*, Mary Shelley's *Frankenstein*, Herman Melville's *Moby Dick*, Hemingway's *The Sun Also Rises*, and Margaret Mitchell's *Gone with the Wind*. [12]

Stories wouldn't be stories without dramatic turns, but not every turn is the same. Not knowing which way things are going keeps us on the edge of our seats, in business as in the theater. That may never have been more true than at the debut of an oratorio called *The Creation* by Franz Joseph Haydn, composed in the late 1790s. Haydn set out to create a soundtrack of the biblical account found in the first chapter of Genesis that, to use a modern idiom, blew the minds of audiences of the day.

Haydn began the piece using rhythmically unstable and hard-to-follow harmonic patterns, including various mini-melodic phrases that trail off into nowhere, meant to depict the chaos of the world before creation. As the narrator and chorus sing through the first few verses of the chapter, their mournful tone reflects the darkness that was over the face of the deep until the moment in which God says, "Let there be light." A single beat of silence follows, then slowly and gently, the chorus sings, "And . . . there . . . was . . . LIGHT." In an instant, everything changes as every instrument in the orchestra joins together to proclaim in a clear, exclamatory C major triad the glory of the light as it's brought to life. It's loud. It's momentous. And it all reverberates around a single, magnificent chord.

This is only one moment in a much longer piece, but Haydn masterfully composed it for the explicit purpose of providing his audience with a sublime aesthetic experience. "Sublime meant something a little different in the eighteenth century than it does today," says Mat Langlois. "It was a state of astonishment where one's soul and mind are forced into a kind of suspension, chasing every other emotion out of one's body. That's literally how they thought about it at the time." Listen to Haydn's piece and you can feel the same thing today (be sure to turn up the volume).

Sublimity was the immediate outcome of a literal turn within this singular musical composition. But the piece also created lasting change. It was one of the few works from Haydn's era that continued to be played long into the nineteenth century, and it set a kind of benchmark for other composers such as Ludwig van Beethoven, who was a student of Haydn and who would go on to surpass his mentor in many ways, becoming the cultural forefather of all romantic music.

Two centuries later another couple of musical geniuses—John Lennon and Paul McCartney—used music in ways no one until that time had. The Beatles were the first rock-and-roll band to forego performing and become strictly studio artists, for example. Incorporating Indian influences in rock music was also unheard of when George Harrison introduced the idea in 1965. Says Harrison:

> I went and bought a sitar from a little shop at the top of Oxford Street called Indiacraft—it stocked little carvings, and incense. It was a real crummy-quality one, actually, but I bought it and mucked about with it a bit. Anyway, we were at the point where we'd recorded the "Norwegian Wood" backing track and it needed something. We would usually start looking through the cupboard to see if we could come up with something, a new sound, and I picked the sitar up—it was just lying around; I hadn't really figured out what to do with it. It was quite spontaneous: I found the notes that played the lick. It fitted and it worked.[13]

The following year, The Beatles released their groundbreaking concept album, *Sgt. Pepper's Lonely Hearts Club Band.* It was a watershed moment in terms of technological and sonic technique and showcased a turn other bands soon followed.

Interestingly, there's some debate about whether The Beatles were the first to do a concept album; *Pet Sounds* by The Beach

Boys preceded it, and competing with The Beach Boys seemed to preoccupy The Beatles in their early days. But *Sgt. Pepper* was the album to which every other band that produced a concept album owed a debt of gratitude, and every band from the late 1960s on couldn't help but be influenced by the Fab Four. You don't get U2 without The Beatles, for example, and you don't get Coldplay without U2. Just as Haydn led to Beethoven, Sir Paul led to Bono, who led to Chris Martin; each turn in music leads to another.

We don't often think of bands as businesses, but few were as industrious as The Beatles, releasing thirteen albums in only seven years. You might say they were a good example of the Protestant work ethic, which by that time had become a cultural norm of which they may have been blissfully unaware. The proverb says, "The hand of the diligent will rule," and The Beatles certainly ruled the charts in their era, collecting twenty *Billboard* No. 1 hits. In fact, on April 4, 1964, the top five songs on the *Billboard* chart were all Beatles tunes: "Can't Buy Me Love" was No. 1, followed by "Twist and Shout," "She Loves You," "I Want to Hold Your Hand," and "Please Please Me." That feat has never been topped.

Unfortunately, by 1970, The Beatles had called it quits, and despite each of the band's members going on to have successful solo careers, the world of music lost something. John, Paul, George, and Ringo all topped the *Billboard* charts as solo acts (Paul nine times); imagine what they might have accomplished had they stayed together.

Breaking up the band wasn't an option in Doug Pruitt's mind as he fought to get Sundt back on track. Just as mercantilist governments once thought wealth was measured in precious metals, the previous leadership at Sundt had believed corporate wealth could be measured in hard, but depreciating, assets. Leading up to its troubles, the company had accumulated row upon row of bulldozers, scrapers, backhoes, and other heavy equipment that wasn't being utilized efficiently, sitting on a dozen acres of land next to an expensive maintenance facility staffed with highly paid mechanics. It was a huge cost center that required millions of dollars a year to operate, and that's why Pruitt made the decision to sell 60 percent of it. When he did, he was met with "big waves of resistance throughout the company."

The idea would be to keep only what the team could put to work at a high utilization rate, carefully calibrated to the nature and expense of each type of equipment. Pruitt decided that Sundt would no longer maintain a maintenance facility or a staff of mechanics, enabling them to sell the land to help reduce debt. Whatever equipment they needed for surges in demand they would rent—at a higher short-term cost but resulting in better overall profitability.

Pruitt also consolidated two tool and supplies warehouses that had been within a hundred miles of one another, selling a lot of the excess inventory and freeing up one of the warehouses so it could be rented to another company. He also sold additional land holdings the company wasn't using and poured the money into training and technology. "It may seem drastic to some, having to fix, close, or sell such a large number of assets in such a short period of time," Pruitt said, "but it's still a business overall. We should have a certain expectation of what an asset should produce for us. And if it does not, it must be fixed, closed, or sold. No exceptions."[14]

In short order Sundt had turned its balance sheet around, paid off the debt that at one time amounted to 120 percent of the company's net worth, and built a cash cushion. "We made more money in one year than we made in the ten years prior," Pruitt said. Training and newfound management discipline led to consistent improvements in revenue and profitability, with the top line nearly doubling over the course of the first four years under his helm. "I think it sent a message that this can work," he said.[15]

By "this" he meant Sundt's strategic planning process, which was helping the company be less opportunistic and remain focused. "You need to define where you're going, and why—that's the strategic side," he says. "And then you need to have excellent tactical plans of how you make that work." Those plans, and the investments in training people to execute them, were paying off.

Change is often unpopular, and of the company's forty-eight most senior managers when Pruitt became CEO, only fourteen remained four years later. But the company had new people in new positions taking on new responsibilities with much success. "A very positive outcome of the turnaround," says Pruitt, "is that we [developed] a high capacity for change, and we learned that this would serve us well as we grew."[16]

Turnaround and change. Change and turnaround. The two are inextricably linked. Not all changes require a complete turnaround, fortunately, and the best way to avoid one is to adopt a mindset of continuous adaptation.

IBM's Thomas J. Watson understood this. "If an organization is to meet the challenges of a changing world," he said nearly a century ago, "it must be prepared to change everything about itself except [its basic] beliefs as it moves through corporate life. . . . The only sacred cow in an organization should be its basic philosophy of doing business."[17]

His corporate great-great-great-great-great grandsuccessor, Samuel J. Palmisano, reflected on Watson's wisdom by noting, "We've lasted 100 years because we never limited ourselves to a view of a particular product,"[18] a perspective shared by modern management guru Jim Collins: "Be prepared to kill, revise, or evolve an idea, but never give up on the company."[19]

There again is the idea of holding tightly to your purpose but loosely to the means by which you accomplish it. It's the difference between journey and destination. We all want to get somewhere, and when we set out toward our destination, we have some idea of how the journey is going to go. But we will inevitably run into unanticipated obstacles. The key is to remain open-minded and flexible so we can adjust on the fly. If we can keep the end in mind, we'll find our way there.

When fast casual restaurant chain Chipotle faced its first major turnaround crisis, it looked to a new CEO who would bring a fresh perspective to the model without messing with the company's mission. Due in part to the chain's rapid expansion, good help became harder to find, and some of its processes showed signs of being outmoded. As a result, several of its restaurants experienced dangerous and much-publicized E. coli and salmonella outbreaks. Not good for a restaurant in the business of serving healthy options to fast food.

"The restaurant managers seemed a little overwhelmed, which is a big problem," said Brian Niccol, the then-incoming CEO of his initial observations. "If the manager isn't confident, that will carry over to the team and show up in poor execution. That wasn't very surprising, because Chipotle has always had a more complicated strategy than its peers have. . . . The food safety incidents were one symptom of that difficulty."

As part of his turnaround plan, Niccol immediately rolled out a new training program, which included explicit directives that the "chefs" taste the food they were cooking. Like a pilot whose own safety is linked to the safety of his passengers, this naturally made them more careful to ensure that what they were serving genuinely was "food with integrity," as Chipotle likes to call it.

Another symptom Niccol observed were the long customer lines, reflective of the chain's growing popularity but frustrating for customers, particularly as they watched Chipotle employees interrupt their assembly line to put together an online order. Niccol's solution was to create an entirely separate operation in the back of the store where additional staff members would focus exclusively on online orders, supported by a new computer system that made doing so easy. This enabled Chipotle to nearly double online sales almost overnight, to a point where they represented nearly half of all revenue.

"Chipotle has illustrated how a business can be revitalized through refocusing on its original core values—in our case, culinary excellence and great customer service," Niccol said. By paying close attention to achieving the changes the company needed from its turnaround while avoiding those it didn't, Niccol helped Chipotle grow to more than six billion dollars in revenue and join the prestigious *Fortune 500*.[20]

Apple is another *Fortune 500* company that every business publication likes to cite for its innovation. One aspect of that about which few consumers are aware is the Apple "squircle," a cross between a square and a circle that Apple uses for all the rounded corners on its products. The squircle makes it impossible to clearly demarcate exactly where the straight lines turn into curves and back, more akin to the curves in a train track than those on a racetrack. The squircle is as distinctive as it is subtle, and it's patented, too.

Apple knows how to make a turn not only *for* its products, but *in* its products. According to *Forbes*, for a period of thirteen straight years (and counting), Apple was the world's most admired company, yet less than 10 percent of its revenue at the end of that time came from products that even existed when it first topped the list. Put another way, more than 90 percent of what Apple offered to the world had turned over in little more than a decade, even as the company retained its place at the height of the corporate food chain. No wonder its "most admired" streak has continued.

One of the secrets of long-standing companies such as Apple and Chipotle is that they understand Say's Law, that supply creates its own demand. None of us knew we needed a smartphone until a smartphone existed. Nobody knew we could get fresh food fast until we could get fresh food fast. Turns are in many ways premised on the hope for a better future. If the road has already been paved for us, there must be a reason. And if it hasn't, paving the way for others can be one of the most meaningful things we can do.

Fundamentally, that's what a free-market economy is all about: creating change by seeking new solutions for problems—even those problems people can't yet articulate. Though nobody ever asked for a microwave oven, it was the right product at the right time, as stay-at-home moms increasingly began entering the workforce in the 1960s and families had less time to cook. And as dated as his thoughts may sound today, Hal Sperlich, who worked alongside Lee Iacocca at Ford and then Chrysler, said, "In ten years of developing the minivan we never once got a letter from a housewife asking us to invent one."[21] Sperlich and Iacocca sensed a need, and filled it.

David Lewis of high-end consumer electronics manufacturer Bang & Olufsen has a similar approach. "I think you can't go out and ask people what they need or want because they don't know," he says. "The whole trick is to come out with a product and say, 'Have you thought of this?' and hear the consumer respond, 'Wow! No, I hadn't.' If you can do that, you're on."[22] As computer scientist and onetime Ernst & Young Entrepreneur of the Year Robert Fraser put it, "Find the most people in the most pain, and solve their problem. The essence of the entrepreneurial spirit is meeting others' needs."[23]

That was an unfamiliar concept in feudal times, when collective submission to an unquestioned authority provided zero incentive for innovation. Everything was structured, everyone had their place, and there was no point in—and perhaps even no thought of—questioning the order of things. But when the religious and economic order began to unravel, so did the feudal system.

Alec Ryrie says, "The kind of socio-political structure that Protestantism engenders—based on free inquiry, participatory politics, and limited government—tends to favor market economics."[24] They wouldn't have called it that back then, but as the concept of wealth began to evolve from land to precious metals to the increasing standard of living brought about by trade, and as a culture of individualism slowly began to emerge, feudalism was doomed.

The changes in religious, economic, and political life were inextricably intertwined. Says Ryrie:

> Three of the key ingredients of the world we live in are rooted in Protestant Christianity. The first is free inquiry.

> Protestants stumbled into this slowly and reluctantly, but Luther's bedrock principles lead inexorably in that direction. This is linked to Protestantism's second, more dangerous contribution: its tendency toward what we are compelled to call democracy. Virtually all Protestants before the 19th century, and many since, regarded that word with horror yet the undertow was there. These impulses have been tempered by the third, much less remarked upon but perhaps more significant, ingredient of Protestantism's modernizing cocktail: its apoliticism. Protestants might have sometimes confronted their rulers, but their most constant political demand is simply to be left alone.[25]

Free inquiry, participatory democracy, and the desire to be left to one's own devices; it sounds like the young nation Alexis de Tocqueville described in his 1835 masterwork, *Democracy in America*. These were among the changes set in motion by the Reformation, ingrained by Enlightenment thinkers, and accelerated by the Industrial Revolution.

Just as the religious realm began to be demarcated from the political, so, too, did the realm of economics. Enlightenment philosophers were the first to differentiate between market forces, which are ultimately beneficial to the common man, and government force, which often ends in tyranny. Adam Smith, for his part, believed government's role should be limited to three major functions: national defense, protection of personal rights, and limited public works such as infrastructure and education, which would enhance the prosperity of everyone but which the private sector did not have proper incentives to provide. The more government could be kept in its place, he argued, the more private enterprise—and the populace it served—could thrive.[26]

Over the course of a few centuries, *rex lex* ("the king is the law") gradually transitioned to *lex rex* ("the law is king"). Economists have since observed that only in an environment in which the rule of law is established and predictable can the polity truly thrive. For some things to change, other things must endure, lest everything become unstable at once. Fundamental to the emerging rule of law were property rights—not only those of landed aristocrats but of anyone, and any property, including the right to benefit from one's own intellectual property. The protection of these rights added torque to this long economic turn leading to the explosion of wealth created by the Industrial Revolution.

Had a feudal serf invented a new type of plow, for example, he would have benefited from it as he cleared the rocks from his nobleman's estate but in no way beyond that. Once he was no longer tied to the land and could retain the rights to the intellectual property he developed, the incentives were there to innovate.

Of course, "intellectual property" would have been as foreign a concept to a serf as "economics" was. When wealth was conceived of only as property, and property as land, only those who had land had wealth. But as the merchant class began to demonstrate that facilitating transactions was itself value creation and that wealth—in the form of precious metals—was fungible, the idea that property rights included the fruit of one's labor broadened this conception. It was then a natural, if protracted, step from the fruit of one's labor extending to the fruit of one's mind.

For centuries, lords of the manor had commandeered the fruit of the labor of those tied to their land, who until that point had no other options. In the same vein, any intellectual property benefits provided by the serf's inventive new plow would have accrued to his lord. But even he would not have been protected from its pilferage. Land was not easily stolen, other than through armed conflict, but ideas were quickly and wholly transmissible, irrespective of the wishes of those who first came up with them.

Why would anyone, therefore, go to the effort of invention—often involving significant and expensive trial and error—without some form of intellectual property protection? They wouldn't, which is why for millennia they didn't, and the world saw precious little innovation. But innovation isn't limited to the realm of physics, and an innovation in law was about to change everything.

An early patent system was first established in the Netherlands in the 1500s, with Britain following in 1624, not coincidentally dovetailing with the Renaissance, Reformation, and Scientific Revolution. Intellectual property was a new concept to the world at that time and didn't gain much traction initially, but in the mid-1700s, as the Enlightenment was spinning up, the number of patents did as well.

Joel Mokyr made the interesting observation that what mattered most to innovation was not how well the actual patent system worked but how inventors perceived it. He cites the example of a man named Richard Roberts, "a prodigiously creative engineer" who testified to a committee of Parliament that but for the patent system he would neither have invented as much as he did nor been confident enough to reveal his innovations to the world.[27] Only a patent gave the independent inventor like Roberts some assurance of security that he could find a manufacturer who would not steal his ideas.

Mokyr says, "This was by no means a universally held view, but it did not have to be. As long as a significant number of would-be inventors believed they had a reasonable chance at hitting a jackpot, some case for an incentive system would be established. In that regard, the economic success of a few famous players would provide the signal needed."[28] The patent system, operating within a relatively stable rule of law, made conditions ripe for innovation, and the Industrial Revolution was on.

Not every turn since then has been helpful; not every change brought about has been good. We can't control or even envision all the downstream consequences (as we'll see in the next chapter) of our turns, but when we come to one, we have no other option but to make the best decision we can. The road may lead to suffering as well as joy, rags as easily as riches. We just can't know. But we still must choose.

One innovation that led to great riches was the steam engine, patented by a Scotsman (and friend of Adam Smith) by the name of James Watt in 1769. Watt did not invent the steam engine, which was originally used to pump water out of coal mines, but by vastly improving both its efficiency and its portability, he was able to secure a patent and greatly expand its applications.

Through a series of twists and turns that would make a terrific movie, Watt had to seek financial backing from a variety of sources until he linked up with Matthew Boulton, a buckles and buttons manufacturer whose metalworking craftsmen could build his machines.[29] Within a few decades, about a thousand steam engines were increasing productivity across a variety of industries in Britain, and Watt and Boulton both became wealthy men.[30]

Steam power was such a game changer because it could be used anywhere, not only close to where raw materials were readily available but close to population centers as well. Presaging today's fears regarding artificial intelligence and how it might bring about a sci-fi nightmare by enabling robots to self-replicate, once steel had been developed, machines could create other machines, from agricultural threshing systems to industrial lathes—turns again begetting other turns. As mercantilism continued to break down, foreign trade loosened up, opening new markets to British and American industrialists.[31]

Another change unleashed by the Industrial Revolution was the concept of the division of labor, famously illustrated by Adam Smith's example of a pin factory. An average laborer in the factory, working alone and using hand tools, might be fortunate to produce ten or twenty pins per day. But by breaking the process down into eighteen different tasks and dividing those tasks among ten specialists, the factory could produce an average of 4,800 pins per worker per day. Henry Ford famously applied this principle to the automotive assembly line, reducing the time it took to build a car from more than twelve hours to a little more than ninety minutes. This not only resulted in less waste and higher quality, it also allowed the average factory employee to be able to afford one of the cars he built.

The rise of factories also changed the relationship between employer and employee, from one of "craftsman and apprentice" to "management and labor." The word *manufacturer* originally meant, simply, "one who manufactures," but it has since come to be associated less with who does the work than who owns the factory. As the scale of factories grew, so did the distance between owner and employee. This has resulted in a host of cascading implications, both good and bad, over the succeeding generations, leading to the employer–employee dynamic we have today—which, with the accelerating trend to remote work, continues to turn in a new direction.

Echoing Tia Kolbaba's reflection on how we can really only see the "moment" of the Reformation by looking back, the Industrial Revolution was largely a revolution in retrospect. It became apparent over time as the pace of new inventions dramatically increased.

Among those inventions, if you can call it that, is the invention of inventors, or what we defined earlier as entrepreneurs. Each new advance of the Industrial Revolution, each new idea brought to life, provided ever-more inspiration that new things can be brought to life, whether they be products, services, or entire new industries and business models. Joseph Schumpeter, the early-twentieth-century economist, was among the first to recognize and celebrate the entrepreneur, or "people who build something out of nothing."[32]

Schumpeter recognized that it is not only inventions that are important but means of production and forms of organization as well. This would include (in his day) not only Thomas Edison and Alexander Graham Bell, but Andrew Carnegie and John D. Rockefeller, and (in ours) not only Steve Jobs and Elon Musk but Jeff Bezos and Charles Schwab—people whom Adrian Wooldridge, political editor of *The Economist*, calls "the Napoleons of their time," who are "thinking on a scale that nobody else in the world is doing."[33] From the steam age to the steel age to the silicon age and beyond, materials may change but the opportunities of inventiveness do not.

That should provide hope to us all. There's an urban legend that all the way back in 1899 the commissioner of the U.S. Patent Office said, "Everything that can be invented has been invented." That's probably untrue, but the 1899 edition of *Punch* magazine did feature the statement in a tongue-in-cheek look at the future, so it was on people's minds.[34] If it's on your mind today, get it out. If there's one defining aspect of humanity, it's our ability to invent. When we come to a dead end, we can always initiate a turn.

Schumpeter coined the term *creative destruction* to describe the relentless march of progress as new innovations cause the old to become obsolete, whether that be technologies, products, services, or business models. As we've seen, creative destruction has always been a reality, but it moved slowly and often imperceptibly for centuries, given the mule-like pace of innovation. But as the Age of Discovery dawned, aided and abetted by the emergence of the rule of law and property rights, the pace of creative destruction picked up steam like one of Watt's old engines.

In one study looking at a twenty-eight-year period of economic growth, economists Steven Davis and John Haltiwanger calculated that while the U.S. averaged a steady and respectable 2 percent net annual growth in jobs, each year some 15 percent of all jobs were destroyed. How could that be? Simple: as 17 percent of jobs are created each year, 15 percent are destroyed. Looking only at the 2 percent growth that nets out from all this creative destruction is like viewing the ocean from the shore on a sunny day; calm and smooth. But underneath the surface, the animals are eating each other.

While no one wants their job to be eaten, creative destruction has been particularly good for consumers, lowering the cost of goods and raising the standard of living far beyond what even the wealthiest early industrialists could have imagined. In fact, Nobel Prize winner William Nordhaus estimated that only a little more than 2 percent of the value of an innovation is realized by today's inventors;[35] the balance is enjoyed across the economy in the form of better products and more affordable prices for all.

That helps explain why more wealth has been created since the millennial generation began than in the previous two hundred years. Statistics from the World Bank show that the number of people around the world living below the global poverty line decreased from 1.9 billion in 1990 to 689 million in little more than a generation.[36] The long turn from feudalism to mercantilism to a market economy resulted in exponentially increasing benefits as it made its way around the world, with each of our businesses playing a small part.

Former chairman of the Federal Reserve Alan Greenspan says if you look at how standards of living have changed over time, it is a "statistical necessity" that the rate of productivity growth was slower in the eighteenth and early nineteenth centuries than it is today,[37] illuminating how creative destruction has accelerated over time. It began to pick up in dramatic fashion following the end of the Civil War, when America's increasing industrial firepower could be directed at things other than literal firepower.

This is a textbook example of the principle that every time we turn *from* something, we're turning *to* something as well. Perhaps many things. Economically speaking, the most significant change coming out of the Civil War was the acceleration of America's evolution from an agrarian to an industrial economy, particularly in the South. Prior to the war, the economy of the South looked more like the rest of the world than that of the North, as the North and Western Europe had been somewhat unique as early adopters of industrialization.

In the mid-1800s most of the global economy had been based on labor-intensive agriculture, much of it tied to slavery. It was the economy of the North which had changed most dramatically since the Founders' time. Economically speaking, says James McPherson, at the start of the war "it was the North that was out of the mainstream, not the South." In the space of a few brief but bloody years, he says, "Union victory in the war destroyed the southern vision of America and ensured that the northern vision would become the American vision."[38]

The most notable and immediate change brought by the turn of the Civil War was, of course, the abolition of slavery. While Frederick Douglass presciently predicted that "the work does not end with the abolition of slavery, it only begins,"[39] the elimination of the evil institution in the U.S. was a real and permanent change, sealed by the Thirteenth Amendment.

Another change was how a war-torn citizenry began to conceive of itself. Prior to the war, Americans tended to refer to the country in the plural, "The United States are . . . " Following the war, this increasingly gave way to referring to the country in the singular, "The United States is . . ."[40] This simple change in plurality signified a change in perspective from conceiving of the nation as a federation of thirty-four distinct states to viewing it as a single union. Federalism has never been the same since.

The war had caused those thirty-four states to come together into two distinct factions, and with the Union victory those two factions would be bound, tensely and imperfectly, into one. As if to seal the change, the assassination of the president of the United States merely days after the war's end—an inconceivable event up to that point in our country's history—stunned the nation.

Seven million Americans lined the tracks to view Lincoln's funeral train as it wound its way through almost two hundred cities and towns on its way to his burial place in Illinois. The following month, some two hundred thousand Union soldiers representing families and communities from Maine to California marched down Pennsylvania Avenue in Washington, D.C. in a somber victory parade.

The war transformed American culture as well. Jay Winik, author of *April 1865: The Month That Saved America*, says,

> By April's end, the country had been changed. Amid the wreckage of war, a kind of universal joint had been shifted, creating one of those rare seismic jolts that history rarely notes more than once a century or even once a millennium. Slowly across the land, in the North as well as the South, a powerful new mood was rising, which would alter the great stream of American—and hence, world—events. In no small measure, this was due, as we have seen, to the actions of a handful of leaders, Union as well as Confederate.[41]

The "powerful new mood" that was arising, slowly yet inexorably, reflects a characteristic of a turn that often goes unnoticed in the moment—the role of momentum.

There is some debate as to what, exactly, momentum is in war, sports, politics, or business. Is it purely psychological, or does it represent some real but unseen force? Entire academic careers have been built around studying that question. But we know it's real in physics; momentum is the product of mass times velocity, and the more momentum an object has, the more difficult it is to stop. You might characterize it as change, in motion.

Sun Tzu, the Chinese master general who lived in the fifth century BC, wrote *The Art of War*, a masterwork that has been studied and cited by military leaders all over the world and throughout history. In it we find one of the earliest references to momentum, described by the author as a "force" or "energy" that stems from a combination of surprise and timing.

We've since learned that when soldiers or athletes perceive that momentum is shifting—positively or negatively—they experience cognitive changes in emotions and motivation as well as physiological changes in heart rate, respiration, adrenaline, and more. Whether or not momentum is real, the *perception* of momentum has real consequences. We're more confident when we feel like we have it.

Perceived momentum is now at the heart of most of my company's consulting engagements. Years ago, "internal marketing" was little more than a catchphrase for employee communications, an afterthought of new corporate initiatives. Since we've learned just how important corporate culture is, however, we've concluded that internal audiences are as least as important as those on the outside.

James Heskett, a professor at the Harvard Business School, says corporate culture can account for up to half of the performance difference between organizations in the same category.[42] Bain & Company's Chris Zook and James Allen say that 85 percent of corporate leaders believe the key barriers they face to sustained and profitable growth are on the inside, and that only 13 percent of employees feel any emotional connection or engagement with their companies.[43] That's a problem just waiting to be solved.

The extent to which companies can create strategic understanding and marshal enthusiasm among their staff is the extent to which a sense of momentum will begin to pervade the company. It's amazing to see what happens when people simply believe it can happen, whatever "it" is. Internal marketing has moved from an afterthought to a strategic priority. If it hasn't yet in your company, it should.

Momentum shifts happened throughout the Civil War, when demoralization among soldiers often meant the difference between life and death. In its early days, the South had the advantage of better military (Robert E. Lee, Stonewall Jackson) and executive (Jefferson Davis) leadership, and it showed up in early victories that disoriented the North. "The Confederates gained the momentum in the summer of '61 at Bull Run," says Derek Frisby. "It stunned the entire country as to what this war was going to be."

The North was surprised, but not defeated, and momentum swings happened throughout the war. Says McPherson, "If the South had its bumblers like Bragg and Pemberton and Hood who lost the West, and Joseph Johnston who fought too little and too late, the North had its McClellan and Meade who threw away chances in the East and its Pope and Burnside and Hooker who nearly lost the war in that theater." Hundreds of thousands died in the back-and-forth struggle.

But over the course of the next two years, the South's early advantages in the eastern theater would be offset by the North's growing capabilities in the west, and by 1863 the Union Army had seized the momentum for good. "Lee lost the ability to take the initiative, which was really his hallmark, after Gettysburg," says Frisby. "That was the last chance. And the momentum of the North proved too much for the Confederacy to effectively challenge. It just had to play out."

By this time Lincoln had equaled, if not surpassed, Jefferson Davis in his capabilities as commander in chief and had found two generals, Ulysses S. Grant in the east and William Tecumseh Sherman in the west, who could finish the job. Further intensifying the momentum of the North was its industrial capabilities, which grew even as the South's resources were diminishing and, thanks to Sherman, increasingly destroyed.

Historian Victor Davis Hanson underscores the importance of momentum in war—and suggests the possibilities it presents in business—saying, "A great general peels the veneer of invulnerability from a winning enemy, and he does so by convincing his own men that victory is entirely within their own purview." Speaking specifically of the "total war" approach Sherman had learned by fighting for his life in pitched battles earlier in the conflict, Hanson says, "By the time [Sherman's] army took Atlanta, it no longer resembled the tentative force that had left Tennessee five months earlier, but felt that it could march through the South with impunity and itself win the war outright."[44]

Momentum, it appears, is based on expectations as much as anything. The advertising industry used to reflect the general business environment, in which the goal was to get as close to perfection as possible. Marketers would conduct reams of research, create a campaign based on their findings, test and improve the ad or campaign, then finally, when they had run out of time (or money), launch it. Today they're increasingly taking a page from the Lean Startup approach, which "favors experimentation over elaborate planning, customer feedback over intuition, and iterative design over traditional 'big design up front' development."[45] Ad campaigns are launched, monitored, and improved in real time. Momentum, in other words, beats perfection.

To be sure, pursuit-of-perfection approaches like Total Quality Management and Six Sigma have their place, particularly when the cost of inconsistency or a breakdown is critically high. But those approaches are designed to improve business outcomes in normal circumstances by significantly reducing the probability that an error or defect will occur, and as a result they require large data sets and often long time frames.

When a company is struggling, by contrast, it's a data set of one. And it's in a hurry. As is often said about families, every company is dysfunctional, but each is dysfunctional in its own way. We once worked with a franchisor that was struggling with increasing competition in a rapidly commoditizing industry. We helped the company clarify its challenge, focus in on a core segment of the market, and refine its brand identity. We put it all together quickly, gave it an intentional kick-start, and watched as the engine began to hum again.

"We couldn't have anticipated the positive effect the rebrand would have had not only on our company, but also on franchise relations overall," the vice president of operations later told us. "Our relationships with our franchisees have done a complete turnaround and the energy here is amazing." *The energy here is amazing.* That's the power of momentum.

There's no such thing in physics or in business as a perpetual motion machine, but that doesn't mean momentum can't be a strategic goal. It's reminiscent of what Daniel Findley said about the importance of accounting for drivers' expectations in roadway design. Interrupt a long, smooth section of road with a sudden, sharp curve and you're likely to catch drivers by surprise, with all its attendant risks. Create a sequence of smaller curves instead, through which drivers can more easily maintain their velocity, and watch people zip through them with confidence. The less dramatic the change in direction, the less likely anyone is to notice, fear, or question it—and the more momentum they can sustain.

It may have been a coincidence that the unwavering belief Sherman had in his troops, and they in him, would lead them to victory in their March to the Sea. It may have been a coincidence that the new management at Sundt turned the company around in part because they believed they could turn it around. And it may have been a coincidence that a ragtag group of amateur college hockey players on the 1980 U.S. Olympic hockey team increasingly believed, as the seconds of the hard-fought third period in the game against the Soviets ticked off the clock, that they could overcome overwhelming odds to win. But if their beliefs led them to fight more fiercely, work more diligently, and skate more aggressively, it made the change they desired that much more likely to happen. In each case, intensity of effort enhanced the momentum of the turn.

Back to the whiteboard. What are the changes with which you're dealing right now, and how can they be viewed in the context of turns? Or, looked at the other way, what changes are or will be manifested by the turns you're navigating now? How can you use the forces at work to cause an effect whose moment has come? How engaged, informed, and aligned is your team? What changes do you want to see come about, and what changes must you prevent, or find a way to cope with? In what direction and velocity is the momentum moving in this moment, and how can it be changed? The bigger and faster the turn, the more consequential these questions become.

The fact that turns result in change is axiomatic. But the change—or changes—any given turn leads to may be anything but obvious, sometimes unexpected, and potentially consequential. And every subsequent turn multiplies those possibilities.

We may think, as we head toward work in the morning, that today will be just another day at the office. What we don't realize is that the detour we take to avoid traffic will give us an idea for how to work around a difficult challenge, the coffee shop on the way is where we'll find our next star employee, and the fender bender we get into will rekindle a relationship with an old friend. It's astonishing to consider all the possibilities that may result from turning this way or that, sooner or later, by ourselves or on behalf of others. We must not allow that to paralyze us, but to the extent it causes us to look both ways, it's helpful to keep in mind.

None of us can influence the outcomes of the turns our companies have already taken. But we can always initiate a new turn, bringing fresh direction to the situations in which we find ourselves. It's best to do that long before the need for a turnaround arises, but even then, there's hope. Turns always bring change, and we can always turn.

> ***The Principle of Change***
> *It's impossible to anticipate all the changes a turn may bring, but it's irresponsible not to consider them. Lean in.*

CONSEQUENCES

"Big wheel keep on turnin' . . ."
Creedence Clearwater Revival

The victory of the U.S. Olympic hockey team over the Soviet Union was the result of a number of factors, including Herb Brooks, a stubborn coach who insisted upon a different approach to recruiting and training his players, a unique and much faster style of play, a challenging road of difficult matches in the months leading up to the Games, and the good fortune that the Winter Olympics that year took place in Lake Placid, New York—home ice. Still, victory was far from assured, and it stunned even the Soviet players, who stood in the middle of the rink as time expired and watched with bemusement the wild celebration of a ragtag group of college kids who had just shocked the world.

Nobody at the time could have imagined the scene that would unfold in Germany only nine years later, as another wild celebration took place amidst the wreckage of the Berlin Wall, marking the beginning of the end of the Communist Bloc. Still, as we watched in real time what was happening on that hopeful November night, one couldn't help but reflect on the events in Lake Placid and think the two were somehow connected. Even seemingly trivial turning points set things in motion that can have unanticipated, enduring consequences.

"The terms and conditions of our lives are set by previous generations and by forces and powers larger than us," says Carl Trueman. "The fall of the Berlin Wall—it was going to happen at some point. Yes, there were key players involved in making it happen at that particular moment, but it was inevitable given the economic crises in the Soviet Union, given the failure of corn and agricultural policy in the '60s in the Soviet Union. It was inevitable that something was going to give in the end."[1] Perhaps the shocking outcome of an Olympic hockey game in a quaint Adirondack Mountain village nine years prior played a small role in making that something give.

Karl Marx, the father of a philosophical model that has led to the deaths of more than a hundred million people, did, ironically, get one observation right. "Men make their own history," he said, "but they do not make it as they please; they do not make it under self-selected circumstances, but under circumstances existing already, given and transmitted from the past." Marx's murderous legacy has been a result of his misunderstanding not only of the circumstances of his time but of human nature itself. Ideas, as they say, have consequences, and bad ideas have victims. But he was right in pointing out that each of us operates in circumstances "given and transmitted from the past." And each of us will transmit into the future those circumstances with which our descendants will have to navigate. That ought to make you think twice.

It has me. As my company works its way through what will likely be a decade-long succession plan, I can't help but reflect upon the failed transition plan that led to our launch. A great deal of time, effort, money, emotion, and—most importantly—

potential ended up being wasted back then, but perhaps not entirely. My business partner and I were determined that, when it came our turn, we were going to do things differently. Today, a new generation of ownership in our firm is working alongside us for the long-term success of the organization, with all negotiations regarding the sale complete and paperwork signed. The two of us are becoming ever-less critical to the company's success, and as we slowly fade into the background, we're confident it will continue to thrive without us.

Turns, like ideas, have consequences, and no turn happens in a vacuum. This is literally the case in roadway design. The safety of a curve depends on a lot of factors, including climate, weather, paving material, time of day, and a host of variable considerations related to both car and driver. But as we've learned, it's also dependent on the location of other curves, the mindset of drivers, and whether they come out of a curve expecting to encounter additional curves. Daniel Findley says that the distance between adjacent curves has been found to be a reliable predictor of collisions.

It's also a bad idea to end a curve on a bridge; while many bridges (including freeway overpasses) are themselves curved, they are designed to have as slow, gentle, and predictable an arc as possible. To design a bridge with multiple, compound curves would be as unwise as it is dangerous. We've learned to design turns in the physical world to have as few negative consequences as possible on what comes next.

But that's much easier to do when you have the reams of data that roadway engineers have collected over the decades. When faced with a new type of turn no one has ever encountered before, it's more difficult to anticipate the long-term consequences. That's common in business endeavors, particularly when new technology is involved.

For example, a generation ago, "space junk" was a meaningless phrase, but now that more than eleven thousand satellites have been launched into orbit from all over the world—up to half of which are now no longer active—there's a lot of stuff floating around out there.[2] Lower earth orbit is a big place, but the launch of each new object increases the danger to the others; the European Space Agency estimates that there are more than a million satellite fragments larger than one centimeter zipping through space many times faster than a speeding bullet, any one of which is able to penetrate the impact shields used by spacecraft.[3] To send up a satellite isn't merely to foster telecommunications, enhance global positioning capabilities, or accomplish any number of other immediate tasks. It's to increase the odds of unfortunate consequences for every other orbiting object.

That's not all that's going on up there. Each year the sun burns off almost five million tons of its matter, lessening its gravitational pull, which means the earth itself is slowly spiraling outward toward the infinite. The good news is that if that weren't happening, the sun would slowly draw our planet inward and we'd eventually get too close for comfort. The bad news is because of the sun's steady loss of mass, we're moving in the opposite direction at a rate of about one and a half centimeters per year.[4] Lest you shudder to consider the implications of that, we're about fifteen trillion centimeters from the sun today, so we should be OK for a while.

That's not to say turns in the natural world don't have real, and sometimes tragic, consequences. Just ask "the wives and the sons and the daughters" of the lost crew of the *Edmund*

Fitzgerald, memorialized in song by Gordon Lightfoot. Caught in an unanticipated tempest "when the gales of November came early," the ship got caught in the perfect storm at precisely the wrong moment; "the searchers all say they'd have made Whitefish Bay if they'd put fifteen more miles behind her." A normal turn in the weather, which those on land experienced as a typical squall in late fall, changed the lives of twenty-nine families forever.

Similar tales could be told about innumerable companies that had to deal with the tempest of the Great Recession, the tidal wave of pandemic-induced government lockdowns, or the riptide of extreme supply chain interruptions. Though not life-and-death situations (in most cases), a lot of livelihoods were lost due to turns beyond their control.

It's impossible to fully appreciate all the consequences of turns such as, say, the taming of fire. Or the invention of the wheel. Or innovations like gunpowder, the printing press, and the telegraph. Each had an immediate impact that was dwarfed by the consequences that followed. The victory of the U.S. Olympic hockey team, the fall of the Berlin Wall, the launch of every satellite, and the tragic sinking of the *Edmund Fitzgerald* all happened at specific places, on specific dates, and at specific times. So did every other seminal event in history.

— A gang of rebels dumped tea into Boston Harbor under the cover of night on December 16, 1775, creating a flashpoint in the run-up to the American Revolution.

— Samuel F.B. Morse sent the first telegraphic message on May 24, 1844, marking the first step of what would become the communications revolution.

- On June 28, 1914, an assassin shot and killed a little-known archduke in a corner of Eastern Europe few people could find on a map, setting off World War I.
- On May 21, 1927, Charles "Lucky" Lindbergh landed in Paris after completing the first solo crossing of the Atlantic, demonstrating the possibilities of global aviation.
- December 7, 1941, will forever live in infamy as the date when the Japanese attacked Pearl Harbor and drew America into World War II.
- The Beatles made their first appearance on *The Ed Sullivan Show* on February 9, 1964, inspiring a generation of rock-and-rollers—and harming the fortunes of barbers everywhere.
- British computer scientist Tim Berners-Lee posted the first rudimentary website on what would become the information superhighway on August 6, 1991.
- On September 11, 2001, terrorists committed the worst attack on the mainland United States since the War of 1812, leading to the global war on terror, the creation of the Department of Homeland Security, the passage of the Patriot Act, and a host of other consequences we are still trying to sort out.

None of the players in the events above could have known what long-term consequences their actions would lead to. They were simply pursuing that which was in front of them at the time. Yet the turns they were part of changed the course of history. That is, at some level, true of every turn we make; heading in one direction precludes all others, sometimes with life-altering results.

I'm reminded of my first-ever professional job, and how I came within a whisker of missing out on it. Shortly after graduating from college, I was working at a health club part-time while I applied for positions in my chosen field, marketing. One day I spotted a newspaper want ad from a hot California advertising agency looking for a field marketing manager based in my hometown to work on the Pizza Hut account. The combination of pizza and marketing sounded like the perfect job for me, so I applied.

Trouble was, when the initial call came in from the woman who would become my boss, it awoke me from a deep sleep. I had been getting up well before dawn to open the health club, and when I got off work at noon each day I'd go home and take a brief nap. She happened to call just when I had entered a dream state, and when I picked up the phone I couldn't get my bearings; I'm sure I must have sounded drunk. Needless to say, the call didn't go well.

After recounting the story that evening to my then-new wife, she encouraged me to send a note to the woman asking for a second chance. I put my pen to paper and not only explained what had happened, but also conveyed my naïve-yet-enthusiastic understanding of marketing and why I was the perfect person for the job. She agreed to give me a second chance and invited me to an in-person interview when she next came to town.

Leaving nothing to chance, I wanted to show how I would take a creative approach to the job and wouldn't let anything stand in my way of success. The day before the interview, I went to a local Pizza Hut and talked them out of a to-go box, to which I attached a handle made of yarn, fashioning it into a briefcase. I printed my resume on the back of a Pizza Hut placemat and made a pen out of a Pizza Hut straw. I even went as far as to pick up a Care Bears hand puppet, which was the kids' toy Pizza Hut was promoting at the time. Carrying my "briefcase" into the interview, I shook my future boss's hand wearing the puppet and pulled out my "pen" and "resume" at the opportune time. My wife later told me she thought I was crazy, but fortunately she didn't say so at the time. I got the job.

A few months after hiring me, my boss told me that there had been people more qualified for the position, but because I took a risk on them, they decided to take a risk on me. It was a lesson I took to heart, and from that point on I decided to always be bold in my work.

Shortly after that, I met the founder of the firm, who told me that my appeal had made its way to his desk, and it was the best business letter he had ever read. That was quite a compliment for a wet-behind-the-ears college graduate, and it seared into my young mind the power of the printed word and fueled my love for writing. That first job eventually led to another, which led to another, then another, then to my launching my own firm and a career as an author. The consequences of that single turn of events led to a life of professional fulfillment on which I could have easily missed out.

We see similar ramifications throughout history. The turns that happened in the mid-1860s not only determined the outcome of the Civil War, they also set in motion consequences we are grappling with to this day. In the summer of 1864, most people, including Abraham Lincoln himself, expected to have a new president after the November election. Lincoln's opponent, George McClellan (the general he had summarily fired after the 1862 midterm elections), was the prohibitive favorite.

The former general had become the Democratic nominee as a result of a compromise between those in the party who favored the war's continuation—McClellan included—and those who opposed it. In exchange for his nomination, his intraparty opponents insisted on inserting a plank in the Democratic platform calling for immediate peace negotiations upon McClellan's victory. Had he won, such negotiations would almost certainly have led to the return of slavery in some form or even permanent secession, in which case the United States would no longer be united states and the great experiment in self-government would have failed.

Fortunately, the turn of events caused by the Union victory at Gettysburg and Sherman's successful March to the Sea gave new hope to both Republicans and pro-war Democrats in the North, carrying Lincoln to victory. Secession was repudiated, the slaves were emancipated, and, as Jay Winik put it, "America would now be something different, not simply a clever political arrangement but a transcendent and pervading idea; it would be a new America, reunited, yes, scarred, certainly, but for the first time, largely whole, looking as much to the future as to the past."[5]

This would have immense long-term consequences. Slaveholders had occupied the office of president for more than two-thirds of the period between the nation's founding and the Civil War, and Southerners ran both houses of Congress for most of that time. Further, more than half of the justices of the Supreme Court prior to the war had been appointed from slave states. But that was about to change.

After the war, no president from a former Confederate state would be elected for more than a century. It would be five decades before leaders in the House or Senate would come from the South, and during that time fewer than 20 percent of new

Supreme Court justices were Southerners. The balance of power in the nation had swiftly and clearly shifted from South to North, as had the power balance between the federal government and the states. James McPherson notes that, "Eleven of the first twelve amendments to the Constitution had limited the powers of the national government; six of the next seven, beginning with the Thirteenth Amendment in 1865, vastly expanded those powers at the expense of the states."[6]

Lincoln's reelection, and Lee's surrender at Appomattox which soon followed, restored the Union and changed Americans' conception of their nation from "these" United States to "the" United States. Since then, the scope of the federal government has grown immensely, strengthening America's place in the world but weakening its federalist character. The constitutional tussle between the powers delegated to the federal government and those reserved to the states has been contested ever since, on issues ranging from interstate commerce to abortion.

Mere months after Lincoln's reelection, the country took another unanticipated turn, the consequences of which have also filtered down to this day. In an attempt to woo pro-war Democrats to the Republican ticket, Lincoln had replaced his vice president, Hannibal Hamlin, with Tennessee senator Andrew Johnson, a former Democrat who was the only senator from a Confederate state to remain in office after his state seceded. Johnson arrived at the president's second inauguration suffering from typhoid fever, exacerbated by the cold and dreary early March weather. The vice president–elect tried to ameliorate his symptoms by downing three glasses of whiskey prior to giving his scheduled remarks, and that's when the trouble began.

An inebriated Johnson stumbled into the Senate chamber and, according to Senate records, rather than giving a traditional brief and polite statement, "rose unsteadily to harangue the distinguished crowd about his humble origins and his triumph over the rebel aristocracy." He was, by all accounts, best described as belligerent, at one point inadvertently revealing that he had forgotten the name of one of the other cabinet members. Johnson ended his exhibition by waving a Bible in the air and kissing it (or as Senator Benjamin Butler of Massachusetts put it, "slobbered the Holy Book with a drunken kiss,") and was unable to complete his duty of swearing in new senators.[7]

Of the event, Michigan senator Zachariah Chandler said the vice president "disgraced himself & the Senate by making a drunken foolish speech. I was never so mortified in my life, had I been able to find a hole I would have dropped through it out of sight."[8]

Senator Chandler was not the only one mortified by Johnson's behavior; the president was as well. "I can never forget President Lincoln's face as he came into the Senate Chamber while Johnson was delivering his incoherent harangue," recalled Secretary of the Senate John Forney. "He took his seat facing the brilliant and surprised audience and heard all that took place with unutterable sorrow."[9]

According to Derek Frisby, Lincoln responded by exiling Johnson from cabinet meetings for a month, and when the vice president arrived late for an important cabinet meeting on April 15 in which General Ulysses S. Grant provided a briefing regarding Lee's surrender, Lincoln refused to let him in. Later that evening the president would be assassinated, his soon-to-be-elevated vice president thus being as uninformed as he was unprepared—and again, apparently, hungover—to step into the top job at one of the most critical moments in the nation's history.

Reconstruction was now in the hands of a man of the South who did not share Lincoln's commitment to restoration "with malice toward none," a turn of phrase that, among many others, underscores why Lincoln is widely considered our finest president. Johnson opposed many of the proposed new civil rights measures and looked the other way at "black codes" that denied fundamentals such as voting rights and public education to freed slaves in former Confederate states. He vetoed the Civil Rights Act of 1866 and the Freedmen's Bureau Bill of 1866, both of which were overridden by Congress and were among the reasons for his impeachment, which fell only a single vote short of the necessary two-thirds majority to convict.

During his brief but consequential tenure, Johnson was responsible for keeping, as Frisby puts it, "a lot of old South in the new South." Lincoln's untimely assassination is one reason why the promises of Reconstruction have often been called a "fabulous failure." No one can say for certain the role this turn of events played in America defaulting for another century on what Dr. Martin Luther King Jr. called "the promissory note" of the magnificent words of the Constitution and the Declaration of Independence insofar as her citizens of color were concerned. We'll never know how much better things may have been, and how much sooner they may have come to pass, had Lincoln served his full second term.

What we do know is that slavery, and all race-based discrimination, is now considered anathema in the civilized world. But it was not necessarily destined to be. Slavery is one of the world's oldest institutions, dating to the earliest recorded history and still practiced in some parts of the world. Based at various times and in various places on race, economic status, or simply as a consequence of having been vanquished in war, it was an ordinary, if malevolent, aspect of human relations. Speaking of America's founding era, historian Seymour Drescher says,

> Personal bondage was the prevailing form of labor in most of the world. Personal freedom, not slavery, was the peculiar institution. In 1772, Arthur Young estimated that only 33 million of the world's 775 million inhabitants could be called free. Adam Smith offered a similarly somber ratio to his students and prophesied that slavery was unlikely to disappear for ages, if ever.[10]

Fortunately, as history continued to turn, Smith's pessimism would prove to be unfounded. "The slow but decisive shift to a Protestant consensus that slavery is intolerable would have lasting effects,"[11] says Alec Ryrie, revealing how the American Civil War is itself one of the consequences of the Reformation. As is America itself. Tia Kolbaba says, "You don't get to 1776 without the Reformation," and as one Pennsylvania pastor intoned on the four-hundredth anniversary of the 1483 birth of MLK's namesake, "If there had been no Luther in Germany, there would have been no Washington in America."[12] We may not be able to draw a straight line from Martin Luther to Dr. Martin Luther King Jr., but we can clearly see that one turn ultimately led to the other.

Megan Armstrong points out that the early communities that were established in New England were all products of the Reformation. Deeply committed believers who had been chafing under sectarian restrictions in Europe braved the seas seeking the freedom to live in concert with their own religious convictions. Later, preachers such as Jonathan Edwards and George Whitefield—who toured the colonies incessantly, in one year traveling some five thousand miles and preaching more than

350 times—informed the cultural and political views of the time, leading to The Great Awakening of the 1730s and 1740s, which set the table for the American Revolution. "The genius of the authors of the United States Constitution," says historian Tom Holland, "was to garb in the robes of the Enlightenment the radical Protestantism that was the prime religious inheritance of their fledgling nation."[13]

When England's King George III increasingly clamped down on the colonists who, by that time, had been bred on self-government for multiple generations, the tension between the authority of the Crown and the independence of the colonies came to a head. The colonists, most of whom had never even visited Britain, were not about to allow the Redcoats to put them under the yoke. So they fought.

We can see how it all comes together. The Civil War represented a violent turn against the age-old institution of slavery, which was the inevitable consequence of a new nation founded on equality, which arose out of an emerging consensus regarding political liberty, which came as a result of many other twists and turns throughout history, including an exasperated friar pounding ninety-five theses onto a church door in Germany. In a very real sense this book wouldn't exist, your company wouldn't exist, and it's possible that you and I wouldn't exist had things not gone the way they did. Turns, indeed, have consequences.

The Reformation had many other long-term effects, of course, not the least of which was the Scientific Revolution. "It was monotheism that launched the coming of physical science," says philosopher Holmes Rolston III, "for it premised an intelligible world, sacred but disenchanted, a world with a blueprint, which was therefore open to the searches of the scientists. The great pioneers in physics—Newton, Galileo, Kepler,

Copernicus—devoutly believed themselves called to find evidence of God in the physical world."[14]

Stephen Meyer hints at how this was, in fact, a consequence of the turns that had come before: "The founders of modern science assumed that if they studied nature carefully, it would reveal its secrets. Their confidence in this assumption was grounded in both the Greek and the Judeo-Christian idea that the universe is an orderly system—a cosmos, not a chaos." He goes on to connect those dots: "A renewed emphasis during the Protestant Reformation on the doctrine of the fall of humankind as well as the fallen state of nature meant that scientists should not take their initial observations of nature at face value. Instead they must 'interrogate' nature using systematic experimental methods."[15]

If God were a god of order, if He had set the world in motion based on discoverable natural laws, and if human beings were rational actors given the freedom to reason for themselves, then political movements and scientific exploration could—and should—be undertaken as expressions of faith. That is indeed what motivated early political philosophers such as Wilberforce, Smith, and Burke, and natural philosophers such as Newton, Galileo, and Pascal. Not all inventors since then have been motivated by faith in God, of course, but belief in discoverable natural laws is a presupposition underlying the innovations of Thomas Edison, Albert Einstein, Bill Gates, Steve Jobs, Elon Musk, and even you and me.

Perhaps the Reformation's most notable consequence is the Enlightenment itself. Tia Kolbaba goes as far as to suggest the latter would not have happened without the former. "That sort of shattering of medieval assumptions, the discovery of the rest of the world, the scientific stuff . . . the Reformation gave us this belief in progress," she says. "They questioned everything."

Kolbaba believes that differentiating the realms of politics, religion, and culture, which we so naturally do today, was an innovation—and a slow-moving one—at that time. Prior to the Reformation, people didn't distinguish between them. "The concept of religion as we talk about it today is modern," she says. "That's not what religion meant then."

Kolbaba even suggests that it was the Reformation that ultimately led to today's increasing secularism, a mind-blowing consequence if there ever was one. "It's oversimplifying," she says, "but thinking about faith as a matter of conscience instead of as a matter of just who you were, that's how we get to separate spheres. One of them has religion in it and the other one has politics in it."

There is a certain hubris in taking for granted the benefits we enjoy today that have come about as a result of turns past. The protection of religion from politics, and politics from religion, that we enjoy in the Western world is a relatively new concept in human history, and by no means guaranteed. Nor is the freedom of speech or the right to vote, which are ours only because of the sacrifices of those who have gone before us. The freedom we enjoy to operate our businesses largely as we see fit is, historically speaking, a new development. Natural, God-given rights though they may be, governments usurping rather than protecting those rights is the historical norm.

Looking back, we can see these developments unfold. The Reformation "confronted Europeans with the fact that Christianity contained radically different truth claims—among Protestants, among Protestants and Catholics, and among all these faiths and Eastern Orthodox Christians," says Ulinka

Rublack, a professor of early modern European history at the University of Cambridge. "This meant that the history of and arguments embedded in truth claims were constantly reconstructed and questioned. Eventually this contributed to the emergence of intellectual positions which recognize religions as cultural systems of meaning and explore their ideas, tensions, and limitations."[16]

Enlightenment thinkers who explored those ideas, tensions, and limitations argued that free enterprise, entrepreneurialism, and trade were the best way to enhance the prosperity of nations, rather than government intervention—up to and including mercantilism. The patent system was a consequence of this line of thinking, as was the development of stock exchanges in the early seventeenth century. For the first time, people could invest in companies they didn't own or operate themselves and benefit from their success. Such investments provided the capital companies needed to innovate and expand more quickly and efficiently, and the increased productivity led to better, cheaper, and more plentiful goods for an emerging middle class.

It also led to a host of unintended consequences, from abusive child labor practices to pollution to the exacerbation of materialism, each addressed in turn by some combination of market forces, government regulations, or changes in cultural norms, with the consequences of each evolution resulting in additional consequences, intended and unintended.

To be sure, economic evolution has had its share of negative ramifications. "This country got strong because of high rates of bankruptcy," says Nassim Taleb, author of *The Black Swan*.[17] But with respect to human flourishing, negative effects have been far exceeded by positive outcomes. In the United States, between 1800 and 2000, real, inflation-adjusted GDP per capita grew from $1,980 to $45,887, a twenty-three-fold increase.[18] Ninety percent of the world's people lived in abject poverty in 1820; today it's fewer than 10 percent.[19] That's why historian Dierdre McCloskey calls the last two hundred years the "Great Enrichment." Over the course of that time the average human being has become wealthier by a factor of twenty-five, the consequences being that "people get food instead of famine, long lives instead of parasites, PhDs instead of illiteracy, high-rises instead of hovels."[20]

Steve Jobs was notorious for many things, one of them being his notable absence from lists of great philanthropists. Jobs ended Apple's corporate philanthropic efforts in 1997, when the company was going through a rough patch, and never brought them back. We don't know, of course, whether and to what extent Jobs quietly gave away money in his private life, but doing so via the company he founded clearly wasn't a priority. Yet we would be hard-pressed to identify a company whose innovations have done more to lift people out of poverty than Apple, not only based on its own products but on countless other innovations by other companies inspired by it.

Wayne Grudem and Barry Asmus, authors of *The Poverty of Nations*, describe the circular chain of events set in motion by a market economy this way: "Trade produces economic gains; economic gains produce higher incomes; higher incomes allow people to buy more goods and services, which leads to even more efficient production, which leads to ever more trade." The consequences of increasingly rapid economic turns over the past two centuries have been dramatic. "Free trade is as close to a perpetual motion machine as any economic idea of man," they say.[21]

Looking back over the past six hundred years, the developed world has moved, albeit in fits and starts, from conceiving of wealth first as land, then as precious metals, then as productive capacity, to today's recognition that wealth is really a function of knowledge; George Gilder points out that the materials to create semiconductors have been with us since time immemorial but, until recently, nobody knew what to do with them. This is why the pace of change continues to gain velocity, with each advance having an accelerating impact on future advances. When one innovator learns something new, it's not long before it's incorporated into the knowledge base of every other innovator.

Thus, with new knowledge comes new waves of change. Here, too, every turn has been interconnected. "The Industrial Revolution depended for its success and sustainability on the prior existence of a series of diverse but connected cultural changes," says Joel Mokyr. "Looking for the Enlightenment as an explanation of the Industrial Revolution just pushes the question back one stage: whence the Enlightenment?"[22] As with the turn toward self-determination, political liberty, and enshrinement in the rule of law that all men are created equal, whether we look backward in time or forward, each economic turn is connected to the others.

Unfortunately, enlightened thinking hasn't always and everywhere carried the day. One benefit of the Cold War was providing a laboratory of comparative economic consequences that could not have otherwise been established; East and West Germany, like North and South Korea today, had identical histories, cultures, religions, geography, and natural resources in the middle of the twentieth century, the difference being the political and economic systems by which they operated. The disparity in economic outcomes was dramatic. "Throughout history, from Venice to Hong Kong," says Gilder, "the fastest growing countries have been the lands best endowed not with things but with free minds and private rights to property."[23]

That's why those of us in business can be down but not out. We may suffer the consequences of previous bad turns, but the free markets, rule of law, and ever-expanding knowledge base that we have inherited from our forebears always enable us to initiate a new turn.

One powerful example of this was the rapid and dramatic change Doug Pruitt and his team were able to bring about at Sundt without needing to wait around for any type of bureaucratic approval. They were not only able to pull the organization out of its tailspin, but also to take steps to ensure it wouldn't happen again. With the company once again on solid footing, Pruitt doubled down on investments in talent, technology, and especially training, hoping to perpetuate the positive consequences his turnaround had spawned.

Sundt instituted two leadership classes, the first for young employees who were only a few years removed from college that focused on three basic aspects of the business and how it functions: estimating, operations, and marketing. The second was a more intensive, three-year program for professionals who were advancing in their careers. It took them on deeper dives into various aspects of business, including cultural dynamics like team building and personality management. The company used an innovative, project-based approach whereby teams of trainees were presented with real-world issues with which Sundt had been struggling and were then charged with developing solutions. Both the organization and those it was nurturing for leadership positions benefited from this approach.

When others in the industry challenged Pruitt about why he was spending so much time and money training people who might end up taking what they had learned to a competitor, he framed his response within the context of its implied consequences: "I'd rather train them and have them go to work for you than not train them and have them stay with me." Echoing Adam Smith, he views what might be seen as a magnanimous approach as being in Sundt's economic self-interest, improving the odds of success for everyone in the industry. "We're all in this together," Pruitt says. "It raises everybody's bar if you can get more training."

One notable bar that such an approach raised was the prosperity of his people. Today Sundt pays not only staff bonuses but also a dividend to its employee owners, and it has gone from a company on the verge of bankruptcy to outperforming the S&P 500 while creating more than one hundred millionaires, only 10 percent of whom are managers. "I've got a warehouse guy who's going to retire and walk out with a very healthy seven-digit number," says Pruitt, proudly. "We'll all do well if the company is doing well. That's what the Sundts were about, and that DNA is still there as part of our company."

To say that Doug Pruitt and his management team orchestrated a successful turnaround at Sundt is a good way of putting it. Orchestration is how composers use turns in composition, instrumentation, tempo, and key to achieve an intended impact upon their audiences. That's what Pruitt and his team did, and their audiences (both clients and employees) were the beneficiaries.

The Beatles orchestrated a turn near the end of "Penny Lane," switching to a higher key to wrap up what one might describe as a melancholy song on an upbeat note. So did The Beach Boys at the front end of "Wouldn't It Be Nice," beginning in one key and unexpectedly—and almost immediately—shifting gears to a harmonically distant one as a way of commanding our attention. Then there's Bon Jovi's rock anthem, "Livin' on a Prayer," in which, three minutes into the song, lead singer John Bon Jovi suddenly launches into a higher key to power up the song's energy level (and make it a karaoke singer's nightmare). All of them used knowledge of their craft to create a turn with delightful consequences, one that hoteliers, restaurateurs, and any company in the experience economy would do well to imitate.

Mat Langlois says one reason composers use turns in music is to create increasing tension that will make the piece more moving, poignant, or exciting. As we all know, this can have consequences beyond the listening ear. If a woeful Billie Eilish song makes you sad as you reflect on your dating relationship, that's a change. If you then go break up with somebody and alter the future of your life, that's a consequence. If jamming to "Free Bird" makes a teenager drive faster, that's a change. If he's playing air guitar in the car and ends up rear-ending someone, that's a consequence.

Movie soundtracks are specifically orchestrated to set the emotional tone for the scenes they accentuate. In most cases the music plays second fiddle to the characters and plot. In others, such as when Whitney Houston changes key three minutes into "I Will Always Love You," or when Celine Dion reaches for the rafters in *Titanic*'s "My Heart Will Go On," it's meant to be the star of the show. Dion's passionate avowal near the end of her paean to love—*You're here, there's NOTHING I fear*—is so overly dramatic that it has become a sardonic meme to underscore the crucial turning point in any plot or narrative.[24]

Turns in music genres also have consequences on those that follow. The ragtime and jazz eras of the early twentieth century led to swing in the '40s and rock-and-roll in the '50s, which in turn evolved into psychedelia in the '60s, hip-hop, heavy metal, and punk in the '70s, hair bands and electronica in the '80s, and grunge in the '90s. And those are only a handful of the dozens of genres that have emerged in the past hundred years or so, each having an influence on others in its own time and beyond.

Consequences, intended and otherwise, have been used to highlight dramatic turns in literature for centuries. *The Lord of the Rings*, the blockbuster movie franchise based on the epic J.R.R. Tolkien trilogy, highlights the story of a good-hearted hobbit named Frodo who has been entrusted with embarking on a long journey to destroy the Ring of Power, which for centuries has corrupted less stout-hearted beings, including Frodo's reluctant companion, Gollum. The story features dozens of dramatic turns and their consequences, all stemming from one, uber-powerful band of gold.

Mary Shelley's *Frankenstein* is another case in point—perhaps *the* case in point. The story of a mysterious scientist and his experiment-gone-wrong has spawned its own idiom regarding things that take on an unanticipated life of their own. Whether it's crowdsourcing a mission statement using a roomful of contributors or a new product development project suffering from endless feature creep, nobody wants to "create a Frankenstein."

Unfortunately, when it comes to science, Frankensteins are sometimes unavoidable. From nuclear weapons to experiments in cloning to invasive surveillance technology, if something can be developed, it will be. Shoshana Zuboff, a professor at the Harvard Business School, cautioned us about the latter decades ago, even before the dawn of the internet. One of her repeated warnings has been that every digital application that can be used for surveillance and control *will* be used for surveillance and control. We've seen that borne out both in the U.S. and abroad, from social media companies to government agencies.

Zuboff also made the prescient case that, "Everything that can be automated will be automated."[25] This has become one of the defining features of the Digital Revolution, which followed on the heels of, and has arguably surpassed in its effects, the Industrial Revolution.

It's difficult to pin down the exact moment when the turn from "industrial" to "digital" began, but it can be traced at least as far back as the 1940s with the invention of the transistor. That, in turn, led to the development of widespread and accessible computing, which led to the internet and mobile telephony, which today has left not a single aspect or element of commerce untouched. Digital advances have made businesses more productive, individuals more connected, consumers more acquisitive, and privacy more elusive. We have gone from the "mechanization of muscle" during the industrial age to the "mechanization of mind" in the digital age, with consequences—good and bad—we've only begun to comprehend.

That's the thing about the consequences of turns. Some are predictable, some not. George Washington refused a crown and stepped down at the end of his second term as president, knowing the likely tragic consequences if America were to be ruled by a monarch or military junta. On the other hand, Benedict Arnold crossed the Hudson River to betray the American stronghold at West Point into British hands, not comprehending what the consequences to his reputation would be. Today Washington's likeness graces both our dollar bill and Mt. Rushmore, while Arnold is the archetype of a turncoat.

In the early 1980s, newly appointed Federal Reserve chairman Paul Volker could have rightly feared going down in history as an economic Benedict Arnold. Volker knew that if he raised interest rates to break the back of what was by then a decade of double-digit inflation, it would throw the country into recession and increase unemployment—perhaps dramatically. But he also knew that once inflation was tamed, the economy could return to healthy growth.

A little more than a year after Volker's courageous action resulted in his being assailed by both sides of the political aisle amidst the worst economic downturn since the Great Depression—unemployment had risen from 6 percent to a peak of more than 10 percent—the economy began growing again. His economic "tough love" had reduced inflation from 12 percent to roughly 2 percent, and for the next quarter century the country enjoyed a steady period of low inflation, high employment, and consistent growth. Volker, like George Washington two centuries before, anticipated both the short- and long-term consequences of the turn he took, and placed his bet on what was prudent rather than expedient.

That's something that tends to separate the turns of teenagers, whose brains have not yet fully developed, from those of adults. Prudence is often the progeny of experience. Putting a thirteen-year-old behind the wheel of a car is not likely to result in a good outcome, nor is giving sixteen-year-olds the right to vote. We all regret decisions we made when our hormones were raging and good judgment had yet to be established; I can think of two separate incidents in which, because of the choices I made as a teen, I could easily have died. The ability to contemplate the potential consequences of our turns is something that comes with time.

Roger Bannister showed a keen grasp of this principle from his early twenties. When he became the first human to best the four-minute-mile mark at age twenty-five, the barrier he broke was not merely one of time but of imagination, inspiring athletes everywhere to aspire to that which had never before been done. He had himself, in fact, been stirred by Sir Edmund Hillary's first successful summit of Mount Everest the year prior. Reflecting years later on his unprecedented athletic accomplishment, Bannister said, "It became a symbol of attempting a challenge in the physical world of something hitherto thought impossible. I'd like to see it as a metaphor not only for sport, but for life and seeking challenges."[26]

Looking back on a lifetime of seeking, and overcoming, challenges, Bannister knew of what he spoke. Always a devoted student, he had skipped the 1500 meters at the 1948 London Olympics to focus on his studies. Four years later, after finishing fourth in that event in Helsinki, he set his mind on being the first to run a sub-four-minute-mile and created a custom training regimen based on what he had learned in medical school. His achievement was therefore not merely one of freakish human capability—though it was that to be sure—but also of imagination and determination.

The consequences to the world of what Bannister accomplished were visible to everyone; among many other accolades he was selected *Sports Illustrated*'s first "Sportsman of the Year." But after another 1500 victory at the 1954 European Championships, he retired from running and never competed professionally. He had already turned his mind to the next challenge, one he considered much more consequential.

Bannister dove headlong into his budding neurology practice, eventually serving as the director of London's National Hospital for Nervous Diseases. Among his many accomplishments there, he led a research effort to develop the first test for steroids at a time when the Soviet Union and other Communist Bloc countries were using them to run up their medal tallies at international competitions.[27] Instead of focusing on his own athletic career, Roger Bannister made it possible for scores of future athletes to achieve their dreams fairly on the field of play.

Thus, when he was knighted by Queen Elizabeth II, it was not for his groundbreaking physical achievements but for his distinguished contributions to the field of medicine. Near the end of his life, Bannister did not hold his athletic accomplishments in higher esteem than his other priorities—quite the contrary. "My medical work has been my achievement, and my family with 14 grandchildren," he said. "Those are real achievements."[28]

Those grandchildren didn't appear out of nowhere, of course, and the satisfaction Bannister felt reflecting on his family didn't just happen. They, too, were consequences of decisions made before and after he left the track. Roger and his wife, Moyra, were married for sixty-three years, from 1955 until his death in 2018, and their fourteen grandchildren were the offspring of their own four children. Their lives took many turns, some more consequential than others.

And they no doubt had their disagreements, a reality all of us face in both our business and personal lives. It's in these circumstances where a better understanding of turns can be of immense and very personal help. We can identify the cause and recognize the contest. We can understand the moment and seek constructive change. Importantly, we can anticipate the consequences and adjust our approach accordingly.

How might the outcome of your next internal argument be different if, instead of shutting it down, you demonstrated an openness to better understanding? How might you impact your company's prospects if you were to volunteer for an unpleasant yet important assignment? What would be the downstream effects in your career of taking a class rather than binge-watching the latest hot show? What might be the outcome of inviting a young person you know out for a conversation over a cup of coffee? Of giving your team an unexpected bonus? Of taking a long-overdue vacation? There's no way of knowing all the consequences unless you do it, and perhaps not even then. But considering the potential ramifications of what might result is valuable to think about.

If the milk in the company fridge has turned sour, it's on us for not checking the expiration date before we stir it into our coffee. If a colleague unfairly attacks us, it's up to us to decide how to respond. Right or wrong, fair or unfair, the situations in which we find ourselves are always the consequence of some past turn of events, and how we respond will have consequences for future turns of events.

We can't know or determine all the consequences any given turn will set in motion. But we're never without responsibility and we have a duty to consider them. When you first learned to ride a bicycle, it wasn't long before you instinctively understood that when you come to a turn you can either lean into it or fly off in the other direction, which will not only injure you but also potentially others. The same is true of every turn. Our decisions today are always and inextricably linked to consequences tomorrow.

> ***The Principle of Consequences***
> *Any turn—good or bad—can reverberate for generations.*
> *Carefully consider the consequences.*

AROUND US ALL

"Turn! Turn! Turn!"
The Byrds

In *Good Strategy Bad Strategy*, Richard Rumelt tells a humorous story about the advanced physics class he took during his college days at the University of California, Berkeley. The course was taught by Nobel laureate Luis Alvarez, who told his assembled students, "This course is labeled 'advanced' because we don't understand it very well. If there were a clear and consistent theory about what is going on here, we would call this course 'elementary' physics."[1]

The same could be said of turns. As instinctive as they can be, fully grasping their import and impact is not so elementary. So what, exactly, are we to make of them?

That question itself is instructive. On one hand it suggests that by becoming more cognizant of turns we can gain a better understanding of their causes and effects. But "what are we to make of them?" implies something else as well: the belief that we can actually *make* something of turns. We can initiate them and we can affect them. We can speed them up and slow them down. We can impact their trajectory and play a role in their resolution. In other words, we're not disinterested observers but active participants in the turns around us.

Through the last seven chapters we've covered a lot of ground. We've talked about the "what" of turns (objects), the "when" of turns (moments), and the "how" of turns (contests). We've looked at the "why" of turns (causes), and "where" turns take us (changes and consequences). The one element we haven't specifically focused on—though it has been woven through each chapter—is the "who" of turns: You. Me. Us.

At the risk of bringing up a painful memory, allow me to take you back to high school English class. It was there we learned that the object of a sentence is what is being acted upon, while its subject is that which is doing the acting. With respect to turns, we are not only objects but also subjects. We get turned—sometimes inadvertently and sometimes intentionally—but we also *make* turns.

Many of the examples we've examined have no human cause; none of us has anything to say about whether the world keeps turning or how electrons spin around the nucleus of an atom. We're simply objects, along with all the other objects in the universe, that move. That said, we humans, uniquely among the animal kingdom, can observe nature's movements, learn about them, and marvel at their role in the order of things. That itself is remarkable.

Even more remarkable, however, is that there are turns about which we do have a say and on which we can have an impact—turns in which we are both subject and object. They aren't just random changes in direction that we must somehow navigate to avoid falling into a ditch or going over a cliff; turns are the stuff of everyday life in which we play a role. Only, however, to the extent that we recognize our ability to do so.

Marcus Tullius Cicero, the renowned Roman statesman and philosopher, said, "What a man sees often he does not wonder at, although he knows not why it happens; if something occurs which he has not seen before, he thinks it a marvel."[2] We see, and effectively ignore, turn after turn in our everyday lives, never pausing in awe of their wonder—whether it's the moon tracing its nocturnal arc across the sky or our astonishing ability to turn on a dime without losing our balance.

Unfortunately, failing to appreciate turns appears to be our default setting. I recently drove nearly the entire length of Interstate 40, a roadway that spans the U.S. from Wilmington, North Carolina, to Barstow, California. Aside from a handful of slight variations in direction, it felt essentially straight. In reality, however, Interstate 40 encompasses many thousands of curves along its cross-country course—turns that are designed to be barely noticeable so that vehicles can safely maneuver at highway speeds. It's one of the reasons the interstate highways are the safest roads in the nation, with a fatality rate nearly half of all other motorways.[3]

In other cases, turns are more dramatic, and notable. I remember sitting in a college class of my own in the early 1980s when a guest speaker, the regional president of a national bank, shared with us the exciting news that his institution was preparing to open branch offices in grocery stores. "What a dumb idea," I thought, the first of many of my predictions that have proven to be wrong.

I recalled that experience when some three decades later my firm was approached by a national jewelry retailer with its plans to, believe it or not, open branches of its own inside grocery stores. "I'm not sure how that's going to work," I admit to thinking, "but I'm not going to make the same mistake twice." We rolled up our sleeves and helped make it happen, and along the way I got a kick out of watching my friends' reactions when I told them about—to their unimaginative minds—the wacky plan.

I love these two examples because they demonstrate entrepreneurship in action. One way to appreciate the long and slow turn from feudalism to free markets is how it has enabled people to help each other in ever more practical ways, such as no longer having to make an extra stop at the bank or mall. New ideas turn problems into solutions. They turn needs into things that fulfill them. As they build upon one another, they turn what used to be lives bound to poverty into freedom rooted in opportunity.

Martin Luther could never have imagined the number, nature, and impact of the turns in which his act of pious defiance would result; it led to more changes in more places over more years than could ever be documented. By contrast, Abraham Lincoln seemed to know exactly what he was getting into when he was elected president, and he understood the stakes better than any of his contemporaries. Some say the Civil War wasn't really about slavery, but instead about whether states had the right to secede from the Union, regardless of the cause. The truth is, it was about both, and Lincoln uniquely grasped that.

Lincoln knew that, should the states settle their differences by splitting up, it would establish a precedent that wouldn't end once the issue of slavery was resolved. If secession was an option, states would have less incentive to settle their differences through democratic debate, and breaking apart would become too easy, much as no-fault divorce laws in our time have led to skyrocketing rates of marital dissolution. At the same time, Lincoln shuddered to consider the wrath due the United States for its historical embrace of slavery.

Years after the Civil War, Stephen Douglas, Lincoln's 1858 debate opponent as the two competed for an Illinois senate seat, realized how wisely the late president had navigated the nation's most consequential turn:

> Had he put the abolition of slavery before the salvation of the Union, he would have inevitably driven from him a powerful class of the American people and rendered resistance to rebellion impossible. Viewed from the genuine abolition ground, Mr. Lincoln seemed tardy, cold, dull, and indifferent; but measuring him by the sentiment of his country, a sentiment he was bound as a statesman to consult, he was swift, zealous, radical, and determined.[4]

Some observers believed Lincoln moved too quickly; others thought he was behind the curve. In fairness, it wasn't entirely up to him. Like Luther at the beginning of the Reformation, there was no way Lincoln could have anticipated, when those first shots were fired at Fort Sumter, all the turns the journey to resolve the issues of secession and slavery would take. But unlike Luther, he clearly grasped the historical moment and his role in it. Things could easily have gone the other way had that singular leader at that distinct time not been there to exercise his exceptional gifts and extraordinary judgment.

But as history would have it, Lincoln wouldn't even have been in that position if it hadn't been for (among many others) Martin Luther and the religious reformers who followed. The stands they took and the examples they set, through a long series of additional twists and turns, contributed to the formation of the United States and the inevitable conclusion, based on its founding principles, that slavery was intolerable.

It's one thing to admire the turns caused by consequential figures in history such as Lincoln and Luther, Isaac Newton, George Washington, and Frederick Douglass. It's quite another to consider the turns made by those who came before them whose names we don't even know.

Newton's mother, widowed three months before his birth, soon remarried and gave young Isaac up to be raised by his grandmother and estranged grandfather for the first decade of his life. When his grandfather died, Newton and his grandmother moved back in with his mother, a half-brother, and two half-sisters.[5] The instability of his family life caused Newton to be lethargic and distracted in school until an uncle took an interest in his education and an attentive schoolmaster took him under his wing. Without their involvement, there's no telling what would have happened to young Isaac.

George Washington's mother regularly read to her children from the Bible and had her son improve his penmanship by copying a book called *The Rules of Civility and Decent Behaviour in Company and Conversation*. When her husband tragically died while George was still a boy, she was unable to ship him off to England to finish his education as the family had planned. Thus, George remained in the colonies and ultimately pursued a military career, a turn of events that would later turn history.

Frederick Augustus Washington Bailey was born into slavery to an unwed mother and unknown father. Just ten years old when his mother died, he was sent to be a domestic servant in Baltimore, where he learned to read and write. Sent back to a plantation from which he ultimately escaped with the aid of a member of the Underground Railroad named Anna Murray, he moved to New York, married Anna, and adopted the last name of Douglass. In addition to helping him escape, Anna worked hard to support the family financially and enable her husband to pursue a career of unprecedented political import.[6]

Frederick Douglass, like George Washington before him, and Isaac Newton before him, could not have appreciated, nor even been aware of, all the turns in the lives of his forebears that would make him who he became. He, like they, couldn't even fully comprehend the turns of which he was a part. But he, like they, was able to initiate turns of his own, and the world is better off as a result.

The grand sweep of history is indeed grand. To think that any of the mundane turns we take in our daily lives could end up being historically consequential is enough to make one shudder. To be sure, most of our turns are something less than momentous, but we can never know what hiring a different person, pursuing a different customer niche, or even taking a different route to work one morning may mean to our future or the futures of our companies.

What we can know is that they will mean *something*. Joe Bunting, the novelist who explained the different types of story arcs in Chapter Six, said, "In life, it can feel like things happen randomly, without causation, and with little or no meaning. The human brain, though, needs meaning. We need to understand why things are going badly for us so we can avoid it or why things are so well so we can do more of whatever's working. This is why humans love story, because stories give us a sense of purpose, meaning, and shape, and they do that through story arcs."[7] With each turn we make—and those we choose not to make—we're writing the stories of our lives.

Zara Altair is the author of the popular *Argolicus Mysteries*, novels set in sixth-century Italy in which her hero, Argolicus, and his tutor, Nikolaos, set out on repeated adventures using their wits and wisdom to right wrongs and champion justice. She says the way to surprise and satisfy readers at the end of a book is to take them to a place where they say, "I never would have guessed." Altair says it's a challenge to keep readers in suspense all the way through a novel, keeping the climax hidden while providing enough foreshadowing to make its ultimate revelation satisfying. "When your story arrives at a twist," she says, "your reader doesn't see it coming, but at the same time, realizes that you've prepared them for [it]."[8]

Brian Andrews, coauthor of the bestselling *Tier One* series of thrillers, explains how to do so. "The key to pulling off an epic twist," he says, "is three-fold: (1) understanding exactly what kind of twist you're trying to pull off, (2) properly controlling the flow of critical information to the reader, and (3) not disappointing the reader by failing to deliver the goods."[9]

He could be talking about corporate strategy there. As we make our plans, it's important to consider exactly what we're trying to pull off, understand as best we can the flow of information around us, and "deliver the goods" for our staff and customers in such a way as to not disappoint them. Tough to do in a mystery novel; even more difficult when you're dealing with the vagaries of the marketplace.

Unlike novelists who have complete control of the plot, characters, timing, and outcomes of their stories—although one survey of fiction authors found that more than nine in ten sometimes feel as if they're somehow taking dictation[10]—in real life we're rarely, if ever, fully in control of our own stories. We can, however, become more adept at anticipating turns our companies may face, understanding their dynamics, and taking a role in determining the outcome.

That includes not only the "what" of each turn, but the "when." Recognizing the moment is a skill that, like fiction writing, can be cultivated. Recall that Daniel Findley explained that in roadway design, one way to understand a turn is as a disruption of equilibrium. In life it seems less that turns are disruptive of equilibrium than that equilibrium is disruptive of turns. When we consider all the days and in all the ways things are turning, it's they that seem continuous, interrupted by brief periods of predictability.

The never-ending cycle of creative destruction is a case in point. New industries are born when a company—or a tinkerer in some garage who hasn't yet formed a company—invents (or stumbles upon) something potentially disruptive. It could be a new machine like the steam engine or the cotton gin, a new process like the assembly line or just-in-time delivery, or a new technology like the semiconductor or blockchain, but whatever it is, it represents a faster, better, and/or cheaper way of helping people accomplish what they wish to accomplish.

When it works, an industry is born. As more customers discover the new product, service, process, or model, the industry enters a period of accelerating growth during which the kinks get worked out, more efficient ways to deliver the goods get figured out, and competitors begin to sniff it out.

The industry then begins to mature. Profit margins grow strong, as do distribution networks and customer relationships, and market adoption becomes broader. Industry pioneers begin to reap the rewards of what they've sown, despite others now horning in on their turf. They also begin to feel the pain of outgrowing their internal systems (or the lack thereof) and the need to build internal cultural institutions to ensure that what they've built doesn't crumble from within. Entropy lurks at every door.

Sooner or later, one too many competing companies enters the market, resulting in too few customers to go around. Each competitor does its best to hold onto as much market share as possible, so price competition heats up. What once was novel has become expected; what once people were willing to pay a premium for is now subject to negotiation. As growth begins to slow and the size of the pie becomes increasingly fixed, players are forced to compete more aggressively for each slice. Good for customers; not so good for product and service providers.

As the cycle continues to turn, companies tend to feel increasingly disoriented, looking for every efficiency they can find as the margin pressure continues. Budgets for training, customer service, and marketing get pinched. Work-arounds grow more frequent as employees seek shortcuts to get done what needs to be done. False starts become common.

Companies at this stage are in many ways just trying to survive. Cultural dynamics begin to deteriorate as staff members lose sight of or confidence in what the organization used to stand for (and probably still touts on its website or in its employee handbook). Office politics begin to get in the way. Gossip grows, as do internal divides. Factions can develop, as differing groups bet on different internal horses and compete for dwindling resources. Decision-making becomes increasingly dysfunctional. Discord becomes the norm.

The best people on staff realize they have other employment options and begin to seek them out. Those who remain can't help but take the company's problems home with them, causing work to infringe upon their personal relationships, which often ricochets right back to the office. A vicious cycle goes full bloom. Lacking some sort of a new disruption, there's nowhere for the company to turn, and most companies at this stage of development (or demise) will go out of business. Inevitably, a new disruption will come along, but if it doesn't arise from within it only hastens an existing company's decline.

You may have recognized your own company's situation in the preceding few paragraphs. Intel's Andy Grove wouldn't be surprised; he described in a nutshell this cycle of disruption when he said, "Success breeds complacency. Complacency breeds failure. Only the paranoid survive."[11] While the last statement is a bit bleak, there's no question that turns are a fact of economic life. No company is immune; those that are unaware of (or blissfully ignore) them as if the current complexion of their market will remain static and predictable are sure to lose. By contrast, those who are alert to the moment can take active steps to stay ahead of a curve that never really stops turning.

Sundt Corporation represented both of those perspectives at different times. Doug Pruitt talks about "decades of arrogance," which set the company up for its near-death experience. "With arrogance comes the tendency to don the blinders and slip into complacency," he says. Being in an industry as dynamic as construction while operating with what he describes as "a laid-back attitude" set the stage for the difficulties that followed. "The trouble that we found ourselves in taught us that as successful as we might be, we can never relax," he says. "We must always look at changes that need to be made or we will fall back into trouble again. As soon as you think you are good enough and lose discipline, you're heading right toward the abyss again."[12]

It wasn't up to Pruitt, and it's never up to us, whether and when the economy might fall into a recession, inflation might take off, or a new competitor might show up and begin eating our company's lunch. But it was up to him, and it is up to us, to anticipate those things happening and make adjustments as warranted. If not, Pruitt says, "you should always expect to pay a penalty. It might not be today, tomorrow, or a year from now, but any period of lapsed discipline has consequences."[13]

And we're back to creative destruction. Companies that lack the discipline to not only execute well on today's business model but also to continually be on the lookout for tomorrow's opportunities risk getting beaten in the transition. A turn in sports again provides a good analogy.

In basketball, teams use the transition offense to take advantage of their opponents' lapse in defensive discipline. It kicks into gear when possession suddenly changes, usually after an errant pass or missed shot. The idea is to quickly push the ball up the court before the defense has time to establish itself and exploit the mismatch. What such a "fast break" requires, however, is not only the players' ability to recognize the moment, but quick decision making, good ballhandling skills, and the confidence that everybody on the team understands their role in the process and their place on the court.

To the average observer, a fast break may look random and opportunistic. For well-coached teams it is anything but. Most coaches consider the transition offense their first and best option as the game rotates from one end of the court to the other, because it can wear down their opponents—mentally and physically—while creating easy scoring opportunities. Their goal is to be in control of the game's frequent turns to the greatest extent possible, creating havoc for the defense.

Havoc, of course, is another word for *entropy*, the tendency of everything in the universe to fall apart. I find it fascinating that the English word *entropy* is derived from the Greek *en-*

tropia, which can be translated as "a turning toward."[14] The notion is one of transformation—in *entropia*'s case, a transformation from order to disorder. Fortunately, there are a lot of other forces that help hold things together—notably, gravity, which can hold together that which entropy seeks to pull apart.

Chapter Five notwithstanding, we don't often think of gravity as a force in turns. After all, gravity keeps our feet firmly planted on the ground but doesn't help us spin upon it. Or does it? Every object on earth has what's known as a center of gravity, which, simply defined, is the point at which the weight of the object is evenly dispersed so that all sides are in balance. Think of the fulcrum of a seesaw, or a pencil balanced on the bridge of your nose. Trucks or buses with high centers of gravity roll over more easily; race cars with low centers of gravity hug the curves.

In human beings, our center of gravity is the center point of our weight distribution. It shifts as we move forward and backward and bend over and straighten up and pick up objects and, yes, turn. Most of the time, we take it for granted, as Cicero observed—we do not wonder at it despite knowing not why it happens. But if a strong gust of wind knocks us off our center of gravity—and perhaps even off the sidewalk—we become immediately aware of it. Toddlers learning to walk are figuring out how to manage their center of gravity. Children learning to ride a bike are doing the same. And businesspeople facing a turn must do so as well. It's not always easy.

My own research shows that companies navigating difficult turns tend to be bedeviled by four internal dynamics that disrupt their centers of gravity. See if you agree that they seem to apply to all of us amid unanticipated turns.

The first has already been mentioned: the challenge of keeping your head on straight—or, for a group, keeping your collective heads aligned. When things are going swimmingly, it's easy for people to overlook minor frustrations and ignore petty disagreements. But when things start to turn, confusion and conflict tend to arise—that which was minor can take on major proportions, and that which was petty can become truly problematic. Things get knocked off balance.

The second challenge is maintaining focus. In a turn, what once was taken for granted—the direction we were heading—is now in flux; what once was a clear path is now a bend around which we can't see. Depending on how quickly things are moving, we must take many considerations into account with little time to do so. Race car drivers risk losing control of their cars. Skiers can easily cross up or catch an edge and find themselves on their backs. Business leaders can lose their best employees, and potentially their companies. Nowhere is focus more necessary than in the turns, yet nowhere are so many competing forces clamoring for our attention.

Related to the need for focus is the necessity of nerve. Turns can be frightening—especially those that are new and unfamiliar. How fast can we take it? Carry too much speed into a turn and you may begin to skid. How cautious should we be? Slow down too much and you may be unable to get your momentum back. What obstacles might be in our way? A delay in recognizing them could be deadly. And perhaps most frightening of all, what, exactly, is around that next curve? Maintaining our footing when we feel our center of gravity shifting requires a confident mind and steady bearing.

Finally, there's the challenge of consistency. Professor Findley taught us that the simplest way to understand a curve is that which connects two tangents. Our goal in a turn, therefore, is to move from one tangent to another with minimal detours. You probably know that the official marathon distance is 26.2 miles, but you may not know that most marathon participants run farther than that. Each course is measured using the most efficient lines through the turns, but most marathoners don't take the most efficient lines, making a difficult race even more difficult. It's axiomatic that a turn represents a break in consistency, but taking wrong tangents only exacerbates the challenge.

These four factors play out in the real world in myriad ways. Remember the Large Hadron Collider, that seventeen-mile loop below Switzerland and France that generates high-impact subatomic particle collisions at unheard-of speeds? Apparently, seventeen miles in circumference and thirteen teraelectronvolts of energy aren't enough. More than 150 universities, research institutes, and industrial partners from all over the world are collaborating on plans to develop a "Future Circular Collider," a one-hundred-kilometer, one-hundred-teraelectronvolt behemoth.[15] This multibillion-dollar investment represents as big a leap in scientific capabilities as it does in scale, and, according to CERN's Gian Francesco Guidice, is "like planning a trip not to Mars, but to Uranus."[16]

As exciting as that might sound, the ability to pull it off is far from certain. All you need to do is look at the Superconducting Super Collider (SSC), a project twenty times the size of the Large Hadron Collider that was at one time under construction circling Waxahachie, Texas. In 1993, after sinking nearly $2.5 billion into the partially completed project, Congress officially lost its nerve and killed it. Nearly fifteen miles of tunnel had been dug and more than two hundred thousand square feet of buildings erected. Two thousand people lost their jobs.

Design of the SSC had begun in 1983 with an original budget of $4.4 billion, more than half of which was to come from foreign governments. By 1993, the estimated cost had risen to more than $11 billion, with precious few checks from other countries having arrived. The Soviet Union, once part of the consortium, was AWOL (to be fair, it was having its own issues in the early 1990s), and relations with Japan, from which the project expected a big investment, had grown touchy because of the U.S. government's pressure to establish import quotas on auto parts. When then-president George H. W. Bush visited Japan to personally seek the funding, he famously threw up on Prime Minister Kiichi Miyazawa at a state dinner. It amounted to a fitting nail in the project's coffin.

One additional factor in the SSC's failure stands out: misalignment among those involved. This wasn't only a problem between governments; a lack of trust between members of the fiercely independent scientific community and those operating in the military culture of the Department of Energy led to repeated conflicts. Even the physicist community was at odds with itself, in part because the significant funding soaked up by such a singular project came at the expense of others.[17]

In retrospect, it's not hard to see why a project as ambitious and unprecedented as the Superconducting Super Collider would have failed; the competing forces were just too powerful for all involved to maintain, or perhaps even find, their center of gravity. But turns can make your company dizzy even if you're not attempting to build a giant, multibillion-dollar infrastructure project.

Strategy, it has been said, is the art of knowing what not to do. There are times we must turn our companies to remain true to what they are and times we must turn them toward change. There are times we must turn things one way (as we do when we're changing a light bulb or car tire, or opening a jar) before turning another. There's at least as much wisdom in knowing when and where to turn as there is in making the turn itself. When two roads diverge in a wood, it's sometimes difficult to decide between them. The more we can understand the signals, the better off we'll be.

Predictability, as we've seen, is a precursor of safe passage, and turns are anything but predictable. When familiar topography is giving way to an unfamiliar landscape, when the curves become unexpectedly sharp or steep, when conditions are less than optimal, when right-of-way is in question, when the road ahead is not well illuminated—all of these elements contribute to making us feel disoriented and afraid.

Assuaging those fears can play a critical role in completing a turn. Winston Churchill, like Lincoln, was the master of the spoken word. In 1940, he lifted the spirits of his war-torn nation with an inspiring paean to the Royal Air Force and its valiant efforts to repel the German Luftwaffe during the Battle of Britain. "Never in the field of human conflict has so much been owed by so many to so few," he mused in what has become one of his most famous quotations. Lesser known is the sentence Churchill uttered just prior to that passage in which he expressed gratitude to the British airmen who, "undaunted by odds, unwearied in their constant challenge and mortal danger, are turning the tide of the World War by their prowess and by their devotion."[18] The valor of the nation's heroes gave courage to its people.

Dr. Stephen Bungay, author of *The Most Dangerous Enemy: A History of the Battle of Britain*, says, "Both Lincoln and Churchill were rooted in the same long western tradition of political rhetoric, and the words spoken by both men at times of crisis have had a profound and lasting impact on their respective nations."[19] Bungay has traced five recurring themes in many of Churchill's speeches. "These themes," he says, "are like leitmotifs which, taken together, spell out his political vision."

First, Churchill paints a picture of a monstrous evil, which is a threat to the entire world. Next, he says not only we, but all of mankind, will be saved if the evil is not permitted to stand. Third, the goal must be nothing less than total victory. Fourth—if you're paying attention to the arc of this story, here's where the turning point comes—the road to victory will be long and hard and involve a great deal of pain and sorrow. Finally, if we stick together and persevere, we can do it. "This was the message he delivered again and again that summer: to Parliament, to the British people, to the occupied countries of Europe, and—crucially—to the United States," says Bungay.[20] Churchill's rhetorical skills, like those of Lincoln, rallied the nation to his cause. Each of us can, to a lesser extent, do the same for our companies.

History, as we've seen, hinges on turns. Orators can turn a phrase that helps a nation turn the tide. Athletes and armies can turn defeat into victory. Composers can turn discordant notes into harmony. Couples can turn rocky marriages into lasting unions. Substance abusers can turn over a new leaf. Businesses can turn the page on their undisciplined past to turn a profit once again. Each of us can turn around, turn back, turn to face the future, or turn full circle—whatever it may take to ensure that things turn out all right in our lives and in the lives of those we serve. *Turn* is both a noun and a verb, an action as well as an outcome. A turn is something we experience, but it can also be something we *initiate.*

True, if you turn a screw too tightly, you can strip it, but if you don't turn it at all it will secure nothing. As cliché as it sounds, the world keeps turning, and each of our companies with it. Our choice is whether to lean in, or to shy away. "Nobody made a greater mistake than he who did nothing because he could do only a little," said the great British statesman Edmund Burke.

Religious wars—real and cultural—still happen. Economic growth isn't always on the upswing. We will never be free of the struggle to create a more perfect union. But over the centuries we've seen sectarian violence decline, unworkable economic models be discredited, and equal opportunity become enshrined in law. The relative economic and cultural stability in which we now operate increases the likelihood that we can continue to create positive change and consequential benefits for those who come after us. The better we become at turns, the better off we all will be.

In a last bit of irony, the meaning of the word *turn* has itself changed over the years. To *turn loose* of something first came into use around the 1590s. *Turning your stomach* dates from the 1620s. *Turnabout* was first used in the 1640s, as was describing a decisive moment as a *turning point*. To *turn in* (go to bed) first showed up in the vernacular around 1690, and people began *turning up* their noses only as recently as 1779. Nobody *turned down* anything until 1891.[21]

Not even the word *turn* is exempt from turns. Thankfully, neither are we. There's a popular expression that describes a deceased person who may not approve of current events as "turning over in his grave." The expression makes sense to us because we all know dead people can't turn. Thus, the turns we face, if nothing else, signify we're alive. That alone is reason to embrace them.

The Principle Around Us All
If we don't like where things are headed, we can always initiate a turn.

TURN PRINCIPLES

The Principle All Around Us
Turns are as commonplace in business as they are in life. The more we understand them, the better we'll navigate them.

The Principle of the Object
Distinguishing that which is turning from the turn itself gives us the critical perspective we need to make levelheaded decisions.

The Principle of the Moment
Every turn has its time. Cultivating the ability to recognize the moment makes us better able to seize it and shape it.

The Principle of the Cause
People aren't the cause of every turn, but we can be a cause in every turn (and often an instrumental one).

The Principle of the Contest
Every turn is a contest of competing forces. You are one of them.

The Principle of Change
It's impossible to anticipate all the changes a turn may bring, but it's irresponsible not to consider them. Lean in.

The Principle of Consequences

Any turn—good or bad—can reverberate for generations. Carefully consider the consequences.

The Principle Around Us All

If we don't like where things are headed, we can always initiate a turn.

ENDNOTES

Introduction

1 Prov. 24:30–32. New American Standard. Bible: 1995 Update.

Chapter 1: All Around Us

1 Alicia Ault, “How Does Foucault’s Pendulum Prove the Earth Rotates?” Smithsonian, February 2, 2018, https://www.smithsonianmag.com/smithsonian-institution/how-does-foucaults-pendulum-prove-earth-rotates-180968024/.

2 Joshua J. Mark, “Aristarchus of Samos,” World History Encyclopedia, February 16, 2022, https://www.worldhistory.org/Aristarchus_of_Samos/.

3 “Facts and History of the Compass,” History of Compass, accessed October 3, 2022, http://www.historyofcompass.com/.

4 “Roger Bannister: First Sub-Four-Minute Mile,” Records, Hall of Fame, Guinness World Records, accessed October 3, 2022, https://www.guinnessworldrecords.com/records/hall-of-fame/first-sub-four-minute-mile.

5 Tia Kolbaba, interview with author, September 30, 2021.

6 Alec Ryrie, *The English Reformation: A Very Brief History* (London: Society for Promoting Christian Knowledge, 2020), Kindle version, 44.

7 Ryrie, *The English Reformation*, Kindle version, 12.

8 Ibid.

9 Megan Armstrong, interview with author, September 14, 2021.

10 Ibid.

11 E Ray Canterbery, A *Brief History of Economics: Artful Approaches to the Dismal Science* (Singapore: World Scientific Publishing Co., 2011), 23.

12 Alan Greenspan and Adrian Woolridge, *Capitalism in America: A History* (Penguin Publishing Group, 2018), 6.

13 Yohuru Williams, “Why Thomas Jefferson’s Anti-Slavery Passage Was Removed from the Declaration of Independence,” History, June 29, 2020, https://www.

history.com/news/declaration-of-independence-deleted-anti-slavery-clause-jefferson.

14 "William Wilberforce," Christian History, Christianity Today, accessed October 3, 2022, https://www.christianitytoday.com/history/people/activists/william-wilberforce.html.

15 Guy Gugliotta, "New Estimate Raises Civil War Death Toll, New York Times, April 2, 2012, https://www.nytimes.com/2012/04/03/science/civil-war-toll-up-by-20-percent-in-new-estimate.html.

16 James McPherson, *Battle Cry of Freedom: The Civil War Era* (New York: Oxford University Press, 2003), Kindle version, 861.

17 Derek Frisby, interview with author, September 13, 2021.

18 Tom Verducci, "The 20 Great Tipping Points," Vault, September 27, 2004, https://vault.si.com/vault/2004/09/27/the-20-great-tipping-points.

19 "Start-Ups for the Long Term: Lessons in Sustainable Growth," News, WARC, November 7, 2019, https://www.warc.com/newsandopinion/news/startups_for_the_long_term_lessons_in_sustainable_growth/42333.

20 Doug Pruitt, interview with author, December 13, 2021.

21 J. Doug Pruitt & Richard Condit, *Level Headed: Inside the Walls of One of the Greatest Turnaround Stories of the 21st Century* (Arizona: Wheatmark, 2014), Kindle version, Location 127.

22 Ibid., 885.

23 Daniel Findley, interview with author, July 28, 2021.

Chapter 2: Objects

1 Nathaniel Scharping, "What Would Happen If the Earth Stopped Spinning?" Discover, March 17, 2021, https://www.discovermagazine.com/planet-earth/what-would-happen-if-the-earth-stopped-spinning.

2 Victoria Barranco and Shira Polan, "What If the Earth Stopped Orbiting the Sun?" Business Insider, November 14, 2019, https://www.businessinsider.com/what-if-the-earth-stopped-orbiting-the-sun-2019-10.

3 "Synovial Joints," Physiopedia, accessed November 26, 2022, https://www.physio-pedia.com/Synovial_Joints.

4 Mat Langlois, interview with the author, December 15, 2021.

5 Mikaela Parrick, *11 Corporate Turnaround Success Stories*, Brown & Joseph, March 6, 2018, https://brownandjoseph.com/blog/11-turnaround-success-stories.

6 David C. Robertson, *Brick by Brick: How LEGO Rewrote the Rules of Innovation and Conquered the Global Toy Industry* (New York: Crown Business, 2013), 102.

7 Fast Company Staff, "The Biggest Business Comebacks of the Past 20 Years," Fast Company, March 17, 2015, https://www.fastcompany.com/3042431/the-biggest-business-comebacks-of-the-past-20-years.

8 Theodore Levitt, "Marketing Myopia," Harvard Business Review, September–October 1975, 1, https://motamem.org/wp-content/uploads/2018/12/Marketing-Myopia-Theodore-Levitt.pdf.

9 Pruitt & Condit, *Level Headed*, Kindle version, Location 241.

10 Jim Collins, "The Flywheel Effect," Jim Collins, accessed October 4, 2022, https://www.jimcollins.com/concepts/the-flywheel.html.

11 Pruitt & Condit, *Level Headed*, Kindle version, Location 107.

12 "Facts & Data on Small Business and Entrepreneurship," SBE Council, accessed October 4, 2022, https://sbecouncil.org/about-us/facts-and-data/.

13 Ibid.

14 Matt Ridley, *The Rational Optimist: How Prosperity Evolves* (New York: HarperCollins Publishers, 2010).

15 Arthur M. Schlesinger Jr., *The Cycles of American History* (New York: Houghton Mifflin Company, 1999), 373.

16 Ibid., 30.

17 "AP US History Notes," Classes, User Files, Warren County Schools, accessed October 4, 2022, https://www.warrencountyschools.org/userfiles/2692/Classes/11541/AP%20US%20History%20Notes%20January%208.pdf.

18 William Lee Miller, *President Lincoln: The Duty of a Statesman* (New York: Vintage Books, 2009), 46.

19 Ibid., 47.

20 Ibid.

21 Ibid., 145.

22 Ibid., 228.

23 Jay Winik, *April 1865, The Month That Saved America* (New York: Harper Perennial, 2001), 375.

24 Miller, *President Lincoln*, 220.

Chapter 3: Moments

1 Eliane Glaser, "Bring Back Ideology: Fukuyama's 'End of History' 25 Years On," The Guardian, March 21, 2014, https://www.theguardian.com/books/2014/mar/21/bring-back-ideology-fukuyama-end-history-25-years-on.

2 Chris H. Luebkeman & Donald Peting, "What Is a Moment?" Architectonics, MIT, accessed October 4, 2022, https://web.mit.edu/4.441/1_lectures/1_lecture5/1_lecture5.html.

3 "How Fast Do Electrons Move Around the Nucleus?," Chemistry, Stack Exchange, May 15, 2017, https://chemistry.stackexchange.com/questions/26501/how-fast-do-electrons-move-around-the-nucleus#:~:text=Plugging%20these%20values%2C%20you%20get,the%20globe%20in%2018.4%20seconds!.

4 Nick Routley, "Visualizing 40 Years of Music Industry Sales," Visual Capitalist, October 6, 2018, https://www.visualcapitalist.com/music-industry-sales/.

5 "CDOT Roadway Design Guide 2018, Elements of Design" Business, Colorado Department of Transportation, accessed October 5, 2022, https://www.codot.gov/business/designsupport/bulletins_manuals/cdot-roadway-design-guide-2018/dg185-ch-03-elements-of-design.

6 Miller, *President Lincoln*, 25.

7 McPherson, *Battle Cry of Freedom*, Kindle version, 857.

8 Gordon Wood, "Notable & Quotable: Gordon Wood on Slavery," Wall Street Journal, November 30, 2021, https://www.wsj.com/articles/notable-quotable-gordon-wood-slavery-1619-project-nikole-hannah-jones-systemic-racism-11638308854?st=nztkgttf66oef8v&reflink=desktopwebshare_permalink.

9 "Have a Proud and Happy Juneteenth!" Juneteenth, accessed October 6, 2022, https://www.juneteenth.com/.

10 Ryrie, *The English Reformation*, Kindle version, 9.

11 Megan Armstrong, interview with author, September 14, 2021.

12 Victoria Coates, "When David Met Lisa," National Review, December 16, 2021, https://www.nationalreview.com/magazine/2021/12/27/when-david-met-lisa/.

13 Carl Trueman, Later Reformation II, Westminster Theological Seminary, https://students.wts.edu/flash/media_popup/media_player.php?id=3912¶mType=audio4

14 John Craig, interview with author, September 3, 2021.

15 Tia Kolbaba, interview with author, September 30, 2021.

16 Ryrie, *The English Reformation,* Kindle version, 59.

17 Donald J. Devine, *The Enduring Tension: Capitalism and the Moral Order* (New York: Encounter Books, 2021), 60.

18 Carl Trueman, "Context of the Reformation II" Westminster Theological Seminary, https://students.wts.edu/flash/media_popup/media_player.php?id=3882¶mType=audio8

19 Ryrie, *The English Reformation*, Kindle version, 12.

20 Ibid., Kindle version, 59.

21 Neil deGrasse Tyson, *Astrophysics for People in a Hurry* (New York: W. W. Norton & Company, Inc., 2017), 75.

22 Stephen C. Meyer, *Return of the God Hypothesis: Three Scientific Discoveries That Reveal the Mind Behind the Universe* (New York: HarperCollins Publishers, 2021), 40.

23 Joel Mokyr, "Economic History and the 'New Economy,'" (speech, National Association for Business Economics, September 12, 2000), Northwestern University, https://faculty.wcas.northwestern.edu/jmokyr/Nabe.PDF.

24 Kevin Maney, *Making the World Better: The Ideas that Shaped a Century and a Company* (IBM Press, 2021).

25 Yulia Razumova, "IBM Centennial Fact-A-Day," Slideshare, accessed October 6, 2022, https://www.slideshare.net/CapCook/summ-up-ibm-centennial-fact-a-dayall.

26 Pruitt & Condit, *Level Headed*, Kindle version, Location 199.

27 Malcolm Gladwell, *Blink: The Power of Thinking Without Thinking* (New York: Little Brown and Company, 2005), 267.

28 George Gilder, *Wealth and Poverty: A New Edition for the Twenty-First Century* (Washington, D.C.: Regnery Publishing, Inc., 2012), 357.

Chapter 4: Causes

1 Matthew Brownstein, "MMO Exclusive: Six-Time All-Star, Moises, Alou," Metsmerized Online, May 22, 2020, https://metsmerizedonline.com/mmo-exclusive-six-time-all-star-moises-alou/.

2 Matt Kelly, "Cubs' Long History of 'Curses'," MLB, October 21, 2016, https://www.mlb.com/news/chicago-cubs-history-of-curses-c206838320.

3 Alec Ryrie, *Protestants: The Faith That Made the Modern World* (New York: Viking Press, 2017), 28.

4 Megan Armstrong, interview with author, September 14, 2021.

5 Ryrie, *Protestants*, 18.

6 Ibid., 2.

7 Sebastian Galiani & Itai Sened, *Institutions, Property Rights, and Economic Growth: The Legacy of Douglass North* (Cambridge: Cambridge University Press, 2014), 164.

8 Ibid.

9 "Francis Bacon, Philosopher of Science," Christian History, Christianity Today, accessed October 10, 2022, https://www.christianitytoday.com/history/people/scholarsandscientists/francis-bacon.html.

10 Galiani & Sened, *The Legacy of Douglass North*, 184.

11 Meyer, *Return of the God Hypothesis*, 48.

12 Galiani & Sened, *The Legacy of Douglass North*, 189.

13 Twice Staff, "Each Man's Life Touches So Many Other Lives," Twice, July 24, 2013, https://www.twice.com/blog/each-mans-life-touches-so-many-other-lives-9547.

14 E. Ray Canterbery, *A Brief History of Economics: Artful Approaches to the Dismal Science* (Singapore: World Scientific Publishing Co., 2011), 44–45.

15 Ibid., 29–33.

16 Ibid., 55–56.

17 Lisa Eadicicco et. al, "The 50 Most Influential Gadgets of All Time," *Time*, May 3, 2016, https://time.com/4309573/most-influential-gadgets/.

18 Matt Blitz, "The Amazing True Story of How the Microwave Was Invented by Accident," Popular Mechanics, September 2, 2021, https://www.popularmechanics.com/technology/gadgets/a19567/how-the-microwave-was-invented-by-accident/.

19 Pruitt & Condit, *Level Headed*, Kindle version, Location 1661.

20 Alex Dopico, "Why Was the Missouri Compromise a Firebell in the Night?" Janet-Panic, June 22, 2019, https://janetpanic.com/why-was-the-missouri-compromise-a-firebell-in-the-night/#Why_was_the_Missouri_Compromise_a_Firebell_in_the_night.

21 First Inaugural Address of Abraham Lincoln, Yale Law School, https://avalon.law.yale.edu/19th_century/lincoln1.asp

22 "Emancipation Proclamation," American Civil War, History, accessed October 10, 2022, https://www.history.com/topics/american-civil-war/emancipation-proclamation.

23 Christopher Flannery, "The American Story", https://podcasts.apple.com/us/podcast/the-american-story/id1474881598?i=100054821937

24 Brad Leithauser, "Love, Death and Music: The Poetry of W.H. Auden," Wall Street Journal, August 12, 2022, https://www.wsj.com/articles/love-death-and-music-review-the-poetry-of-w-h-auden-11660317959.

25 Library of Congress, "'Daisy' Ad (1964): Preserved from 35mm in the Tony Schwartz Collection," YouTube video, 1:20, September 7, 2016, https://www.youtube.com/watch?v=riDypP1KfOU.

26 Lyndon B. Johnson, "The President's Address to the Nation Announcing Steps to Limit the War in Vietnam and Reporting His Decision Not to Seek Reelection," The American Presidency Project, March 31, 1968, https://www.presidency.ucsb.edu/documents/the-presidents-address-the-nation-announcing-steps-limit-the-war-vietnam-and-reporting-his.

27 Kenneth T. Walsh, "50 Years Ago, Walter Cronkite Changed a Nation," U.S. News, February 27, 2018, https://www.usnews.com/news/ken-walshs-washington/articles/2018-02-27/50-years-ago-walter-cronkite-changed-a-nation.

28 Maria_Pro, "The Story Behind 'Dust in the Wind' by Kansas," Ultimate Guitar, December 12, 2017, https://www.ultimate-guitar.com/articles/features/the_story_behind_dust_in_the_wind_by_kansas-70049.

Chapter 5: Contests

1 Richard P. Rumelt, "Strategy in a Structural Break", McKinsey Quarterly, December 1, 2008, https://www.mckinsey.com/capabilities/strategy-and-corporate-finance/our-insights/strategy-in-a-structural-break

2 Universe Today, "What If Earth Stopped Orbiting the Sun?" Phys, July 11, 2016, https://phys.org/news/2016-07-earth-orbiting-sun.html.

3 Fraser Cain, "Galaxy Rotation," Universe Today, May 11, 2009, https://www.universetoday.com/30710/galaxy-rotation/.

4 J. Warner Wallace, "Four Ways the Earth Is Fine-Tuned for Life," Cold-Case Christianity, November 4, 2015, https://coldcasechristianity.com/writings/four-ways-the-earth-is-fine-tuned-for-life/.

5 Andree Seu, "The Next Thing," World, December 3, 2005, 55.

6 George Gollin, "Physics and Dance," University of Illinois in Urbana-Champagne, accessed October 10, 2022, http://web.hep.uiuc.edu/home/g-gollin/dance/dance_physics.html#7.

7 Miller, *President Lincoln*, 152.

8 Ibid.

9 McPherson, *Battle Cry of Freedom*, Kindle version, 855.

10 Winik, *April 1865*, 375.

11 "Friction," Merriam-Webster, accessed October 10, 2022, https://www.merriam-webster.com/dictionary/friction.

12 McPherson, *Battle Cry of Freedom*, Kindle version, 855.

13 Miller, *President Lincoln*, 163.

14 John Yoo, "Democrats and the McChrystal Fiasco," Wall Street Journal, June 24, 2010, https://www.wsj.com/articles/SB10001424052748704629804575324610902472990.

15 McPherson, *Battle Cry of Freedom*, Kindle version, 856.

16 Ibid., 858.

17 Ibid., 855.

18 Ben Cohen and Andrew Beaton, "40 Years Before He Retired, Mike Krzyzewski Was Nearly Fired," Wall Street Journal, April 4, 2022.

19 Ryrie, *Protestants*, 61.

20 Ibid., 84.

21 "Winston Churchill to the Duke of Marlborough, September 29, 1898," The Library of Congress, https://www.loc.gov/exhibits/churchill/interactive/_html/wc0020.html#:~:text=In%201898%20Churchill%20was%20anxious,Sudan%2Dthe%20Battle%20of%20Omdurman.

22 Ryrie, *Protestants*, 22.

23 Ibid., 22.

24 Carl Trueman, "The Reformation", Westminster Theological Seminary, https://students.wts.edu/resources/media.html?paramType=search&keywords=The+Reformation&speaker=12&ScrBook=&ScrChap=&ScrVerse=&ScrVerseEnd=&year=&srch=search, also https://podcasts.apple.com/us/podcast/the-reformation/id924126015?i=1000319521437

25 Ryrie, *Protestants*, 41.

26 Ryrie, *The English Reformation*, Kindle version, 61.

27 Ryrie, *Protestants*, 91.

28 Ibid., 39.

29 Peter Robinson, "'Tear Down This Wall' at 34", Uncommon Knowledge podcast, June 17, 2021, https://uncommonknowledgehoover.podbean.com/e/tear-down-this-wall-at-34/

30 Gilder, *Wealth and Poverty*, 359.

31 Pruitt & Condit, *Level Headed*, Kindle version, Location 1125.

32 Ibid., Kindle version, Location 1119.

33 Ibid., Kindle version, Location 1573.

34 Ibid., Kindle version, Location 1558.

35 Dusan Randjelovic, "11 Most Profitable Sports Leagues—Their Value Will Surprise You," Athletic Panda, June 3, 2020, https://apsportseditors.org/others/most-profitable-sports-leagues/.

36 "Apollo 13, a Successful Failure," The Planetary Society, accessed October 10, 2022, https://www.planetary.org/space-missions/apollo-13.

37 Gilder, *Wealth and Poverty*, 43.

38 David Mamet, "The Tichborne Claimant," National Review, January 24, 2022, 45.

Chapter 6: Changes

1 "Before Don Haskins," Background, The Don Haskins, accessed October 10, 2022, https://thedonhaskins.weebly.com/background.html.

2 Dana Husinger Benbow, "What Texas Western's Black Players and White Coach Did in 1965 Continues to Ripple," Indianapolis Star, February 12, 2021, https://www.indystar.com/story/sports/college/2021/02/12/they-were-the-first-all-black-starting-five-to-win-ncaa-title/4285930001/.

3 Ibid.

4 Ryrie, *Protestants*, 59.

5 Ryrie, *The English Reformation*, Kindle version, 28.

6 Ryrie, *Protestants*, 4.

7 Meyer, *Return of the God Hypothesis*, 26.

8 Robin Barnes, *The Oxford Handbook of the Protestant Reformations* (Oxford: Oxford University Press, 2017), Kindle version, 68.

9 Christopher McFadden, "The Very Long and Fascinating History of Clocks," Interesting Engineering, April 13, 2019, https://interestingengineering.com/the-very-long-and-fascinating-history-of-clocks.

10 Rublack, *The Oxford Handbook of the Protestant Reformations*, Kindle version, 71.

11 Andrew Reagan, "Toward a Science of Human Stories: Using Sentiment Analysis and Emotional Arcs to Understand the Building Blocks of Complex Social Systems," PhD Diss. (University of Vermont, 2017), 87, https://cdanfort.w3.uvm.edu/research/andy-reagan-phd-dissertation.pdf.

12 Joe Bunting, "Story Arcs: Definitions and Examples of the 6 Shapes of Stories," The Write Practice, accessed October 10, 2022, https://thewritepractice.com/story-arcs/.

13 "The Beatles and India," The Beatles Bible, August 9, 2009, https://www.beatlesbible.com/features/india/.

14 Pruitt & Condit, *Level Headed*, Kindle version, Location 1664.

15 Ibid., Kindle version, Location 1838, Location 1875.

16 Ibid., Kindle version, Location 2025.

17 Jim Collins, *Built to Last: Successful Habits of Visionary Companies* (New York: HarperCollins Publishers, Inc., 1994), 81.

18 T.Calkins, *Defending Your Brand: How Smart Companies use Defensive Strategy to Deal with Competitive Attacks* (Palgrave Macmillan, 2012), 101.

19 Collins, *Built to Last*, 29.

20 Brian Niccol, "The CEO of Chipotle on Charting a Culinary and Digital Turnaround," Harvard Business Review, November–December 2021, https://www.exed.hbs.edu/Documents/assets/hbr-ceo-chipotle-charting-culinary-digital-turnaround.pdf.

21 Gary Hamel and C.K. Prahalad, "Seeing the Future First," Fortune, September 5, 1994. https://archive.fortune.com/magazines/fortune/fortune_archive/1994/09/05/79699/index.htm

22 Deborah Steinborn, "Talking about Design," Wall Street Journal, June 23, 2008 https://www.wsj.com/articles/SB121372804603481659

23 Robert E. Fraser, *Marketplace Christianity: Discovering the Kingdom Purpose of the Marketplace* (Overland Park, Kansas: New Grid Publishing, 2004), 77.

24 Ryrie, *Protestants*, 4.

25 Ibid., 2–3.

26 Peter J. Boettke, "economic system," Britannica, accessed October 10, 2022, https://www.britannica.com/topic/economic-system.

27 Joel Mokyr, "Intellectual Property Rights, the Industrial Revolution, and the Beginnings of Modern Economic Growth," American Economic Review 99, No.2 (2009): 352.

28 Ibid., 353.

29 Martin Hannan, "This Is How James Watt Started the Industrial Revolution," The National, April 29, 2019, https://www.thenational.scot/news/17603647.james-watt-started-industrial-revolution/.

30 Canterbery, *A Brief History of Economics*, 66.

31 Ibid., 67.

32 Alan Greenspan, Adrian Wooldridge, and Abby Joseph Cohen, "Lessons for the Future: A History of Capitalism in America," October 18, 2018, https://www.cfr.org/event/lessons-future-history-capitalism-america.

33 Ibid.

34 Dennis Crouch, "Tracing the Quote: Everything That Can Be Invented Has Been Invented," Patently-O, January 6, 2011, https://patentlyo.com/patent/2011/01/tracing-the-quote-everything-that-can-be-invented-has-been-invented.html.

35 Matt Nesvisky, "Who Gains from Innovation?" National Bureau of Economic Research, No. 10, October 2004, https://www.nber.org/digest/oct04/who-gains-innovation.

36 World Bank, Poverty and Shared Prosperity 2020: Monitoring Global Poverty (Washington, D.C.: World Bank, 2020), 32. https://openknowledge.worldbank.org/bitstream/handle/10986/34496/9781464816024_Ch1.pdf.

37 Greenspan & Wooldridge, *A History of Capitalism in America.*

38 McPherson, *Battle Cry of Freedom*, Kindle version, 861.

39 Winik, *April 1865*, 380.

40 Ibid., 379.

41 Ibid., 377.

42 Sean Silverthorne, "The Profit Power of Corporate Culture," Working Knowledge, Harvard Business School, September 28, 2011, https://hbswk.hbs.edu/item/the-profit-power-of-corporate-culture.

43 Interview with Chris Zook, "The Founder's Mentality: Leveraging Startup Thinking for Long-term Growth," Knowledge at Wharton, July 21, 2106.

44 Victor Davis Hanson, *The Savior Generals: How Five Great Commanders Saved Wars That Were Lost – From Ancient Greece to Iraq* (New York: Bloomsbury Press, 2013), 243.

45 Steve Blank, "Why the Lean Start-Up Changes Everything," Harvard Business Review, May 2013, https://hbr.org/2013/05/why-the-lean-start-up-changes-everything.

Chapter 7: Consequences

1 Carl Trueman, "The Reformation", Westminster Theological Seminary, https://students.wts.edu/resources/media.html?paramType=search&keywords=The+Reformation&speaker=12&ScrBook=&ScrChap=&ScrVerse=&ScrVerseEnd=&year=&srch=search, also https://podcasts.apple.com/us/podcast/the-reformation/id924126015?i=1000319521353

2 Nibedita, Mohanta, "How Many Satellites Are Orbiting the Earth in 2021?" Geospatial World, May 28, 2021, https://www.geospatialworld.net/blogs/how-many-satellites-are-orbiting-the-earth-in-2021/.

3 Jon Sindreu, "The Difficult Search for Dangerous Space Junk," Wall Street Journal, November 11, 2022, https://www.wsj.com/articles/the-difficult-search-for-dangerous-space-junk-11668162607.

4 Greg Jacobs, "Milo's Solar System: Quantitative Replacement for the PHET 'My Solar System' Orbit Simulator," Jacobs Physics, December 31, 2020, https://jacobsphysics.blogspot.com/2020/12/replacement-for-phet-my-solar-system.html.

5 Winik, *April 1865*, 383.

6 McPherson, *Battle Cry of Freedom*, Kindle version, 859.

7 Jennifer Errick, "The Drunken Veep," National Parks Conservation Association, January 2, 2018, https://www.npca.org/articles/1720-the-drunken-veep.

8 Jonathan R. Allen, "Andrew Johnson Drunk at Lincoln's Second Inaugural," Civil War History and Stories, The Civil War, accessed October 10, 2022, http://www.nellaware.com/blog/andrew-johnson-drunk-at-lincolns-second-inaugural.html.

9 Errick, "The Drunken Veep."

10 Dan McLaughlin, "American Slavery in the Global Context," National Review, January 24, 2022, 20–21.

11 Ryrie, *Protestants*, 7.

12 Tia Kolbaba, interview with the author, September 30, 2021.

13 Joseph Loconte, "Tom Holland in Dominion: How the Christian Revolution Remade the World, as Cited in A Brief History of Individual Rights," National Review, December 27, 2021.

14 Meyer, *Return of the God Hypothesis,* 25.

15 Ibid., 24.

16 Rublack, *The Oxford Handbook of the Protestant Reformations*, Kindle version, 3.

17 "Nassim Taleb on Covid Misconceptions, Fed Policy, Inflation," Bloomberg video, 49:24, September 22, 2020, https://www.bloomberg.com/news/videos/2020-09-22/nassim-taleb-on-covid-misconceptions-fed-policy-inflation-video.

18 "Real GDP per Capita, 2011 US Dollars," Human Progress, accessed October 10, 2022, https://www.humanprogress.org/dataset/maddison-project/data-table/.

19 "Hammond Reviews Ten Global Trends in Economic Affairs", Human Progress, August 25, 2020, https://www.humanprogress.org/alexander-hammond-reviews-ten-global-trends-in-economic-affairs/.

20 Deirdre Nansen McCloskey, "The West Didn't Steal Its Way to Wealth," National Review, December 27, 2021.

21 Wayne Grudem & Barry Asmus, *The Poverty of Nations, A Sustainable Solution* (Wheaton, IL: Crossway, 2013), 268.

22 Galiani & Sened, *The Legacy of Douglass North*, 173.

23 Gilder, *Wealth and Poverty*, 315.

24 Toxinn, "This Song Makes Every Scene Better," YouTube video, 6:19, October 10, 2016, https://www.youtube.com/watch?v=lXfEPZl75E0; Greatwhodini, "Sports Moments with Titanic Song," YouTube video, 5:56, January 18, 2018, https://www.youtube.com/watch?v=c19Q9wB8v6Y.

25 Pukar C Hamal, "Everything that can be automated will be automated . . ." Medium, June 3, 2015, https://medium.com/@pukar/everything-that-can-be-automated-will-be-automated-5058249c00d4#.

26 Rabbi Benjamin Blech, "Roger Bannister and Breaking the Four Minute Mile", Aish.com, March 6, 2018, https://aish.com/roger-bannister-and-breaking-the-four-minute-mile.

27 Jason Daley, "Five Things to Know About Roger Bannister, the First Person to Break the 4-Minute Mile," Smithsonian Magazine, March 5, 2018, https://www.smithsonianmag.com/smart-news/five-things-know-about-roger-bannister-first-person-break-four-minute-mile-180968344/.

28 Randy Lilleston, "Why Roger Bannister Was a British Hero," AARP, March 5, 2018, https://www.aarp.org/politics-society/history/info-2018/roger-bannister-obit-fd.html.

Chapter 8: Around Us All

1 Richard Rumelt, *Good Strategy Bad Strategy, The Difference and Why It Matters* (New York: Crown Publishing Group), 193.

2 Blaise Pascal, *Pensees* (Thoughts) (digiREADS Publishing, 2018), 32.

3 "Interstate Frequently Asked Questions," Highway History, U.S. Department of Transportation, Federal Highway Administration, accessed October 10, 2022, https://www.fhwa.dot.gov/interstate/faq.cfm#question17.

4 Miller, *President Lincoln*, 307.

5 "Isaac Newton," MacTutor, accessed October 10, 2022, https://mathshistory.st-andrews.ac.uk/Biographies/Newton/.

6 "Frederick Douglass," US History, accessed October 10, 2022, https://www.ushistory.org/people/douglass.htm.

7 Bunting, "Story Arcs."

8 "How to Work Twists, Turns, and Reveals in Your Mystery," Writing Craft, Zara Altair, accessed October 10, 2022, zaraaltair.com/twists-turns-and-reveals-in-your-mystery.

9 Ibid.

10 Jim Davies, "How Do Some Authors 'Lose Control' of Their Characters?" Literary Hub, December 18, 2019, https://lithub.com/how-do-some-authors-lose-control-of-their-characters/.

11 Jorma Ollila, "Intel's Andy Grove and the Difference Between Good and Bad Fear," Financial Times, April 11, 2016, https://www.ft.com/content/4c84d2e8-fa5f-11e5-8f41-df5bda8beb40.

12 Pruitt & Condit, *Level Headed*, Kindle version, Location 2264.

13 Ibid., Kindle version, Location 2208.

14 "Entropy," Online Etymology Dictionary, accessed October 10, 2022, https://www.etymonline.com/word/entropy.

15 "Future Circular Collider," CERN, accessed October 10, 2022, https://home.cern/science/accelerators/future-circular-collider.

16 Davide Castelvecchi, "Physicists Lay Out Plan for a New Supercollider," Nature, January 15, 2019, https://www.scientificamerican.com/article/physicists-lay-out-plans-for-a-new-supercollider/.

17 David Appell, "The Supercollider That Never Was," *Scientific American*, October 15, 2013, https://www.scientificamerican.com/article/the-supercollider-that-never-was/.

18 Winston Churchill, "The Few" (speech, London, August 20, 1940), International Churchill Society, https://winstonchurchill.org/resources/speeches/1940-the-finest-hour/the-few/.

19 Dr. Stephen Bungay, "His Speeches: How Churchill Did It," International Churchill Society, April 6, 2009, https://winstonchurchill.org/resources/speeches/speeches-about-winston-churchill/his-speeches-how-churchill-did-it/.

20 Ibid.

21 "Tour," Online Etymology Dictionary, accessed October 10, 2022, https://www.etymonline.com/word/tour?ref=etymonline_crossreference#etymonline_v_15418.

INDEX